Stopwatch

Teacher's Guide

4

Geraldine D. Geniusas

Richmond

Richmond

58 St Aldates
Oxford
OX1 1ST
United Kingdom

Stopwatch Teacher's Guide Level 4

First Edition: September 2016
ISBN: 978-607-06-1247-3

© Text: Geraldine D. Geniusas
© Richmond Publishing, S.A. de C.V. 2016
Av. Río Mixcoac No. 274, Col. Acacias,
Del. Benito Juárez, C.P. 03240, México, D.F.

Publisher: Justine Piekarowicz
Editorial Team: Suzanne Guerrero
Design Team: Jaime Angeles, Daniel Mejía
Pre-Press Coordinator: Daniel Santillán
Pre-Press Team: Susana Alcántara, Virginia Arroyo,
Daniel Santillán
Cover Design: Karla Avila
Cover Photograph: © **Thinkstock.com** mezzotint
(female sprinters start)

Richmond publications may contain links to third party
websites or apps. We have no control over the content of these
websites or apps, which may change frequently, and we are
not responsible for the content or the way it may be used with
our materials. Teachers and students are advised to exercise
discretion when accessing the links.

The Publisher has made every effort to trace the owner of
copyright material; however, the Publisher will correct any
involuntary omission at the earliest opportunity.

Printed in Brazil by Forma Certa
Lote: 775883

Cod: 292712473

Contents

Scope and Sequence

Unit	Vocabulary	Grammar	Skills
0 **Who are we?**	**Review:** daily routines, food and drink, free-time activities, transportation **Parts of the Body**	Present simple; *Going to;* *Will;* Time expressions (present and future); Information questions with *wh-* words	**Listening:** Identifying statements and responses
1 **What do you celebrate?**	**Celebrations:** birthday, blow out candles, get a diploma, graduation, Independence Day, make resolutions, New Year's Eve, open presents, set off fireworks, watch a parade, wave flags, wear a cap and gown	Present continuous (future meaning)	**Reading:** Making a mind map **Listening:** Understanding a description of a holiday **Project:** Making a holiday infographic
2 **How are you feeling?**	**First Aid:** antiseptic spray, bandages, burn gel, first-aid kit, ice pack, medicine, thermometer **Symptoms and Injuries:** bruise, cut, fever, headache, runny nose, sore throat, stomachache, sunburn	*Should;* Short answers; Zero conditional	**Listening:** Taking notes to identify main points and supporting examples **Reading:** Reading a magazine article **Project:** Making a fact sheet
3 **How can we save the planet?**	**The Environment:** conserve water, plant trees, pollute the environment, recycle, reduce carbon emissions, save electricity, send garbage to landfills, use clean energy, use fossil fuels	First conditional	**Reading:** Identifying opinions **Writing:** Giving reasons to support your opinions **Project:** Making a minidocumentary
4 **What's your passion?**	**Fan Activities:** be a fan of, be good at, collect action figures, dress up as characters, get an autograph, put on face paint, put up posters, stand in line, wear a hat, wear team colors	Intensifiers; *Already, Yet*	**Reading:** Understanding questions in a dialogue **Speaking:** Asking questions as an active listener **Project:** Making a *Fan Activities* brochure

Unit	Vocabulary	Grammar	Skills
5 **How much do you remember?**	**Personal Experiences:** buy a lot of souvenirs, fall in love, forget, get in trouble, get lost, have a lot of fun, make a mistake, take care of **Keepsakes:** baby tooth, drawing, necklace, seashell, toy car	Past continuous; Short answers; Past continuous and past simple: *When*; Past continuous: *While*	**Reading:** Making connections between images and text **Listening:** Completing an outline **Project:** Making a personalized timeline
6 **What do you need to travel?**	**Travel:** book a flight, catch a train, exchange money, get a passport, hire a guide, pack a suitcase, stay in a hotel **Collocations:** get hot, get hungry, get lost, get ready, get started, get there, get thirsty, get up	Present perfect; Short answers; Present perfect: *Ever*; Present perfect: *Already, Yet*; *Been, Gone*	**Reading:** Reading images **Listening:** Identifying images from descriptions **Project:** Making a *Travel Experience* poster
7 **How adventurous are you?**	**Extreme Sports:** kite surfing, mountain biking, rock climbing, skydiving, snowboarding, white water rafting **Adjectives:** bored, boring, excited, exciting, interested, interesting, terrified, terrifying, thrilled, thrilling, tired, tiring	*Might*; *Would*; Present perfect: *Never*	**Reading:** Understanding text organization **Writing:** Classifying facts **Project:** Making an *Adventure Profile*
8 **What do we have in common?**	**Habits:** go out to eat, hang out, keep a journal, order take-out, sleep in, stay up late, stream movies, work out	*Too, Either*; *So, Neither*; *Me too, Me neither*	**Listening:** Identifying speakers **Reading:** Reading a blog **Project:** Conducting a *Social Acceptance* survey

The Concept

Stopwatch is a motivating, six-level secondary series built around the concept of visual literacy.

- *Stopwatch* constructs students' language skills from A0 to B1 of the Common European Framework of Reference (CEFR).
- A stopwatch symbolizes energy, speed, movement and competition and gives immediate feedback. The *Stopwatch* series offers dynamic, engaging activities and timed challenges that encourage students to focus and train for mastery.
- *Stopwatch* has a strong visual component to facilitate and deepen learning through authentic tasks, compelling images and the use of icons.
- The series was conceived for the international market, with a wide range of topics, incorporating cultures from around the world.

- The six-level framework of the series allows for different entry points to fit the needs of each school or group of students.
- The syllabus has been carefully structured. Each level recycles and expands on the language that was used in the previous books. This process of spiraled language development helps students internalize what they are learning.
- Each level of *Stopwatch* covers 90 – 120 hours of classroom instruction, plus an additional 20 hours of supplementary activities and materials in the Teacher's Guide and Teacher's Toolkit.

The Components

Student's Book & Workbook

Units are divided into distinct spreads, each with a clear focus:

- A **Big Question** establishes the central theme of the unit and promotes critical thinking, curiosity and interest in learning.
- **Vocabulary** is presented in thematic sets and with rich visual support to convey meaning.
- **Grammar** is introduced in context, enabling students to see the meaning, form and use of the structure.
- **Skills** (reading, listening, writing and speaking) are developed through engaging topics.
- **Culture** invites the learner to immerse oneself in the rich variety of cultures and peoples on our planet.

- **Review** activities provide consolidated practice for each of the grammar and vocabulary areas.
- In the **Project**, students apply the skills they learned in the unit to a creative task built around the Big Question.
- **Just for Fun** is a page with fun activities that teachers can assign to fast finishers.
- The **Workbook** pages offer extended practice with the vocabulary, structures and skills of the unit.
- **The Student's Audio** contains all the listening material in the units.

Teacher's Guide

Brief instructions or summaries provide a quick guide for each Student's Book activity, including **answer keys** and **audio scripts**.

A fun and engaging **warm-up** activity reviews previous knowledge and prepares students for what will be seen in each lesson.

A **wrap-up** task practices newly-learned material. Warm-ups and wrap-ups usually take the form of games.

Extension tasks promote use of language in communication and real-life situations.

Digital options provide alternatives to the projects using electronic media.

Specific questions, related to the Big Question of the unit, stimulate critical thinking.

Teaching tips help develop and enrich teachers' skills.

Teacher's Toolkit (printable materials)

The **Teacher's Toolkit** is a comprehensive resource that is available on the Richmond Learning Platform <https://richmondlp.com>.

It includes the Class Audio and Worksheets

Worksheets

- Grammar Worksheets (2 per unit) with Answer Key
- Reading Worksheets (2 per unit) with Guidelines and Answer Key
- Vocabulary Worksheets (2 per unit) with Answer Key

It also includes Project Rubrics, Score Cards, Tests and Test Audios

Project Rubrics

- These contain proposed criteria that can be used to evaluate students' performance in the completion of the unit projects.

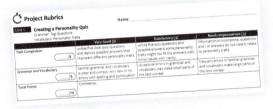

Scorecard

- These help students evaluate their progress by reflecting on their newly-acquired grammar, vocabulary, reading and listening skills.

Tests

- **Placement Tests** (Beginner & Intermediate) with Grading Scale and Answer Key

These will help teachers assess students' level of English on an individual and group basis and select appropriate tests.

- **Standard Tests** (1 per unit) with Answer Key

These cover the vocabulary and grammar from the units, as well as reading and listening skills.

- **Tests Plus** (1 per unit) with Answer Key

These are the **extended** version of the Standard Tests, which include an additional communication component designed to assess speaking and writing.

- **Mid-Term Tests** with Answer Key

These should be given out after having completed U4.

- **Final Tests** with Answer Key

These should be given out after having completed U8.

The Big Question: What do you celebrate?

• Student's Book & Workbook

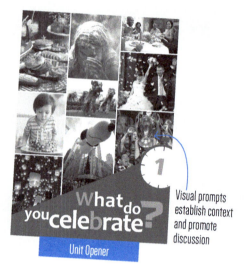

Visual prompts establish context and promote discussion

Unit Opener

Vertical orientation of some sections to conform to visual requirements

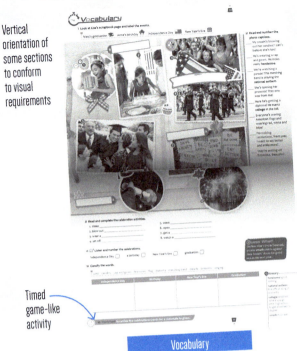

Timed game-like activity

Vocabulary

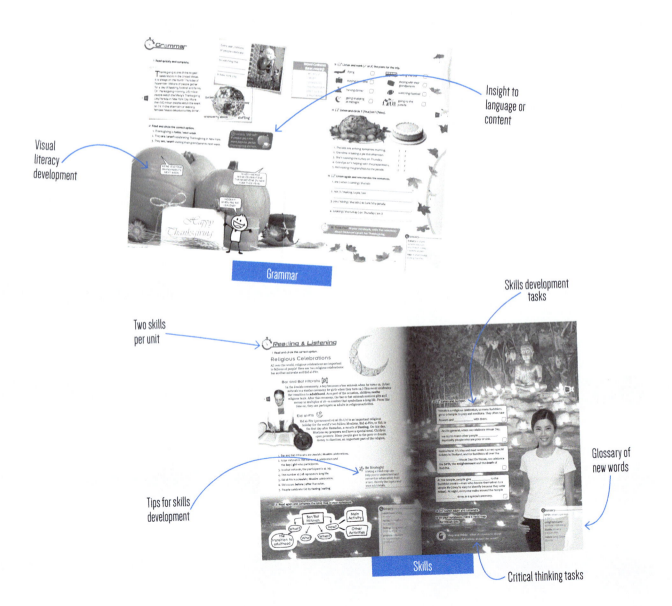

Visual literacy development

Grammar

Insight to language or content

Two skills per unit

Tips for skills development

Skills development tasks

Glossary of new words

Critical thinking tasks

Skills

• Student's Book & Workbook

Content relevant to students' lives

Level-appropriate language encourages learner engagement

Audios available on the platform and in the Digital Book

Culture

Critical thinking / Value tasks

Sample of the project

Linguistic and conceptual preparation for the project

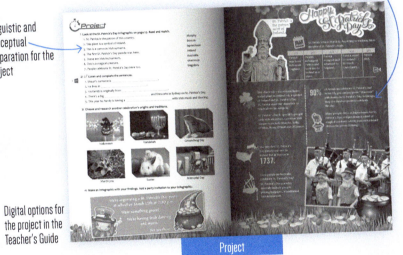

Project

Activities for fast finishers

Just for Fun

Digital options for the project in the Teacher's Guide

More practice with unit grammar and vocabulary

Topics expand on the unit theme

Review

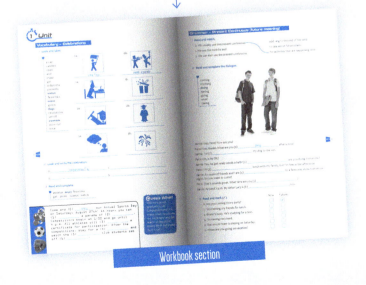

Workbook section

Who are we?

► 10

Grammar	**Vocabulary**

Present Simple: Pam <u>hates</u> bananas. Betty <u>doesn't</u> <u>like</u> carrots and lettuce.

Going to: <u>I'm going to</u> get up soon.

Will: <u>I'll</u> close the window.

Time Expressions: She <u>always</u> gets up early. He <u>never</u> eats breakfast. They <u>sometimes</u> do homework. He <u>often</u> goes to the gym.

Information Questions with *Wh-* Words:
<u>What</u> did they use? <u>Where</u> did they live? <u>When</u> did they live there? <u>Why</u> were they short?

Review: daily routines, food and drink, free-time activities, transportation

Parts of the Body: arm, brain, brow ridge, cheekbone, face, foot, freckles, hair, hand, head, leg, nose, skin

Listening

Identifying statements and responses

Who are we?

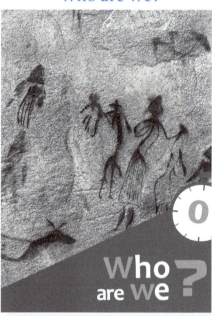

In the first lesson, read the unit title aloud and have students look carefully at the unit cover. Encourage them to think about the message in the picture. At the end of the unit, students will discuss the big question: *Who are we?*

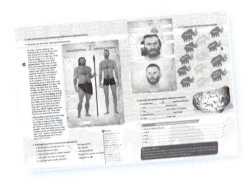

 **Teaching Tip**

Setting the Right Tone

Among the many things you'll want to do on the first day of class is set the tone that you'll carry throughout the year. Here are some tips to follow on the first day of class and all year:

• Be likeable. Don't be afraid to smile to create that human connection.

• Be calm. This does much to settle first-day jitters, as well as allowing your students to focus on you and their learning.

• Be clear. Present all material with simplicity. Pause often and make eye contact. Don't forget to model.

• Be confident. When giving instruction, tell your students only what they need to know. Be direct and concise.

• Be fun. Your students will take their cue from you, so if you want them to enjoy themselves, you need to as well.

Lesson 1

Student's Book pp. 8 and 9

Objectives

Students will review the **Present Simple** and **Time Expressions** as well as **Free Time**, **Routines** and **Transportation** vocabulary to talk about activities and preferences. They will also review *going to* for future plans and *will* for spontaneous plans.

Warm-up

Students play a game called *Two Truths and a Lie* as an ice-breaker.

- Say three statements about yourself: something you like, something you don't like and a dream you have. Two are true but one is a lie.

- Students guess which is the lie.

- Students form groups of three and play the game with information about themselves.

1 Look and complete the descriptions of each person.
Students use the fact cards to complete sentences about each person.

Answers

1. never eats breakfast, hang out with friends, walks, carrots and lettuce, travel to Rio de Janeiro, 2. does homework, likes drawing, takes a bus, like milk, is to travel to Italy, 3. goes to the gym, loves camping, always goes … by car, hates, His dream is to travel to the Grand Canyon

2 Read and write the name of the person from Activity 1.
Students read the statements and identify which person from the previous activity would say each one.

Answers

1. Betty, 2. Tom, 3. Pam

Extension

Students play a game of *Ten Questions*.
- Students form groups of three or four.

- Each student chooses one person from Activity 1.

- Others in the groups take turns asking up to ten *Yes-No* questions to find out who the person is.

Wrap-up

Students play a guessing game to consolidate the lesson.

- Students write a passage about themselves, based on the texts in Activity 2.

- Collect the passages and redistribute them.

- Students guess who wrote the passages.

(No homework today.)

Teaching Tip

Learning Students' Names
Knowing students' names is important for classroom management, and also to express that each student is a valuable part of the class.

- Review students' names before you enter the classroom. Make a note of students who have the same first name, or of names you aren't sure how to pronounce.

- Greet students as they enter the classroom, if possible. Introduce yourself and ask their names.

- Repeat students' names every time you refer to them. If you cannot remember, ask their name again.

- Have students make name tags for the first few lessons.

Unit 0

Warm-up

Students reflect on and write about their skills in English.

- Ask *What are you good at in English? What do you need more help with? What topics are interesting? How can you use English in real life?*

- Tell students to answer the questions on a sheet of paper. Explain that you will collect them, to keep the information in mind as you teach this level.

3 🎧¹ **Listen and number the photos.**

Students listen to the conversations and match each to the appropriate photo. Have students read the *Guess What!* box.

Answers

left to right 2, 3, 4, 1, 5

Audio Script

0. KATE: Hi, Andy.
   ANDY: Hi, Kate. Ready to study?
   KATE: I think so. I can't believe the big test is tomorrow.
   ANDY: I know!
   KATE: Brrr. It's cold in here.
   ANDY: Oh! I'll close the window.
   KATE: Thanks!

1. DENISE: What did you do yesterday, Jackie?
   JACKIE: I went shopping for my prom dress.
   DENISE: Did you find one?
   JACKIE: I did.
   DENISE: You have to show me. What does your new dress look like?
   JACKIE: I'll draw it for you. And then, after school, you can come to my house and see it. It's like this…

2. MOM: Hello? Oh. A fever? I see. I'll come to get him, then.
   TEEN BROTHER: Who was that?
   MOM: The school called. Robby is sick.
   TEEN BROTHER: I'll pick him up.
   MOM: That's OK. I'll go. I might need to take him to the doctor.

3. SAMANTHA: Hey, Dave, your girlfriend Mandy's birthday is tomorrow.
   DAVE: Oh, no! I completely forgot!
   SAMANTHA: Uh oh. What are you going to get her?
   DAVE: I'm not sure… I know! I'll bake her a cake!
   SAMANTHA: Well that's original.
   DAVE: Hey! You know she loves cake!
   SAMANTHA: That's true. I'm sure she'll love it.

4. VERONICA: I went to see Grandma today.
   TODD: Oh, how's she doing?
   VERONICA: Not too well. I think Grandma is lonely.
   TODD: That's not good. I'll visit her this afternoon.
   VERONICA: I think she'd like that.

5. RILEY: Hey, Zack. Did you see that new sci fi movie, *Robot Attack*?
   ZACK: No. I was really busy this week.
   RILEY: It's a good movie. You should see it!
   ZACK: I'll try to see it on the weekend.
   RILEY: It's great! Let me know what time you're going. We can go together!

---

4 🎧¹ **Listen again and match.**

Students match the statements with the responses using *will* from the listening.

Answers

1. I'll draw it for you. 2. I'll pick him up. 3. I'll bake her a cake. 4. I'll visit her this afternoon. 5. I'll try to see it on the weekend.

Extension

Students role-play situations to review the form and use of *will* for spontaneous plans.

- Students form pairs. They act out the situations in Activities 3 and 4. Encourage them to add details.

- Come together as a class and have some volunteers act out their role play for the class.

Wrap-up

Students play *Charades* to review vocabulary.

- Divide the class into three or four groups.

- One student in each group acts out an activity from Activity 3 for the others to guess.

- Groups repeat with different volunteers acting out the vocabulary.

▐▐▐▶ **(No homework today.)**

Objectives

Students will read and listen to information about humans and Neanderthals. They will be able to use **Parts of the Body** vocabulary. They will also review **Information Questions with *Wh-* Words**.

Warm-up

Students preview vocabulary with a game called *Call My Bluff*.

- Write the vocabulary from the glossary on the board and number it 1 to 4.
- Students form four groups.
- Assign a word to each group and give students the correct definition from the glossary.
- Groups think of another definition for their words.
- Groups read their words and the two definitions aloud. Other students guess which is the correct one.

5 Look at the pictures and circle the main differences in their appearance.

Students compare the bodies of a Neanderthal and a modern human.

Answers

Answers will vary.

6 Read the text and check. Then label the body parts.

Students read the text about Neanderthals and check their ideas from the previous activity. They use the words in blue to label the body parts in the illustrations.

Answers

body, top to bottom arm, hand, legs, feet
faces, left column head, skin, brow ridge, nose
faces, right column brain, freckles, hair, cheekbones

7 Read again and match the questions and answers.

Students match questions and answers about the text in Activity 6.

Answers

1. During the Ice Age. 2. Yes, they did. 3. Because they needed more heat. 4. No, they weren't.

Extension

Students role-play an interview.

- Students form pairs. One student is the interviewer and the other is a scientist who studies Neanderthals.
- The interviewer asks questions similar to those in Activity 7, and the scientist answers.
- Encourage students to try to not look at their books.

Wrap-up

Students listen to descriptions and identify the part of the body.

- Say *It's a part of the body that helps you to think.* Elicit the body part: *the brain.*
- Give other descriptions to elicit the names of the body parts on pages 10 and 11.

(No homework today.)

Unit O

Warm-up

Students make a Venn diagram to compare information.

• Draw a Venn diagram on the board like this:

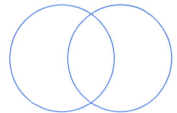

14

• Students form pairs and draw a Venn diagram.

• In one circle, they write as much information as they remember and can find in the Student's Book about Neanderthals. I the other circle, they write about modern humans. Where the circles intersect, they write what the two have in common.

• Have pairs share their Venn diagrams with other pairs.

8 🎧² Listen and circle the verbs you can hear.

Students identify past tense verbs used in the listening.

Answers

lived, made, spent, used buried, took care of, painted, played, found

---

Audio Script

REPORTER: With us today, anthropologist Roman Rock, an expert on the Neanderthals.
Welcome to the studio, Roman.
ROMAN: Thanks for the invitation.
REPORTER: Please tell us what anthropologists have discovered about Neanderthals so far.
ROMAN: Yes, there are still a lot of mysteries, but we know some interesting facts about them.
First of all, they lived at the same time as early humans, so we can't call them ancestors. Secondly, they lived not only in caves, but also in huts. They made them with branches and mammoth bones. Of course they spent a lot of time in caves to protect themselves from the cold—it was the Ice Age after all!
REPORTER: (laughs) Yes, not surprising. That is why sometimes we refer to them as cave men. But they knew how to make fire, right?
ROMAN: That's right! We know they knew about fire, but we don't know what they used it for. Some evidence shows they didn't use it for cooking!
They were very similar to humans. They made fire, buried their dead and took care of their sick. They used sophisticated tools, too.
REPORTER: What about their free time? Any discoveries?
ROMAN: Oh yes! They painted. There are paintings on cave walls to prove it. And they played music, too! Scientists found a small flute in a cave in Slovenia in 1996.

---

9 Complete the sentences using the verbs from Activity 8.

Students complete sentences with past simple verbs.

• Have students read the *Guess What!* box.

Answers

1. used, 2. painted, 3. took care of, 4. buried,
5. played

10 Think Fast! Change the sentences in Activity 9 into questions.

Students do a three-minute timed activity: they form questions using the sentences in the previous activity as prompts.

Answers

1. did they paint, 2. did they take care of in sickness, 3. did they do with their dead,
4. they play music

Extension

Students conduct research on Neanderthals.

• Students form groups of three or four.

• Assign, or let students choose, topics to research.

• Encourage students to use visual aids.

• Students present their findings to the class.

Wrap-up

Students quiz each other on a reading to consolidate the lesson.

• Students form pairs and think of two more questions about the reading.

• Students form new pairs and quiz each other on the reading, using the questions from Activity 10 and their own questions.

➡ **(No homework today.)**

1 What do you celebrate?

Grammar	Vocabulary

Grammar

Present Continuous (Future Meaning):
We're visiting your grandparents next week. I'm not baking a pie tomorrow. When are we leaving?

Vocabulary

Celebrations: birthday, blow out candles, get a diploma, graduation, Independence Day, make resolutions, New Year's Eve, open presents, set off fireworks, watch a parade, wave flags, wear a cap and gown

Reading	Listening

Reading

Making a mind map

Listening

Understanding a description of a holiday

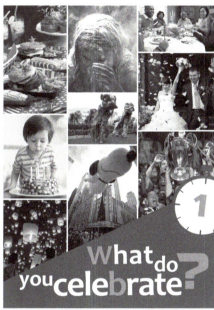

What do you celebrate?

what do you celebrate?

In the first lesson, read the unit title aloud and have students look carefully at the unit cover. Encourage them to think about the message in the picture. At the end of the unit, students will discuss the big question: *What do you celebrate?*

🌧 Teaching Tip

Eliciting Information from Students

Instead of giving them information, ask your students to provide it. When a student asks a question like *What does this mean?* say something like *That's a good question—what do you think?* Encourage the student and others in the class to express their thoughts. Students can often answer their own questions, or at least begin to.

There are a number of benefits to eliciting, including tapping into previous knowledge, building students' confidence and fostering learner independence. Some students may not be used to eliciting. However, if you work eliciting into your lessons on a regular basis, even something as simple as asking for today's date from your students, they will most likely begin to offer you answers even before you ask.

Vocabulary

Objective

Students will be able to use **celebrations** vocabulary to talk about holidays and other celebratory occasions.

Lesson 1   Student's Book pp. 14 and 15

Warm-up

Students start thinking about the big question.

- Draw students' attention to the photos on page 13 and ask *What are they celebrating?* Then draw their attention to the title of the unit. Read it aloud and ask *What do you celebrate?*
- Elicit answers, but don't worry about accuracy.
- Ask students to brainstorm other events that they celebrate. Write them on the board.

1 Look at Lisa's scrapbook page and label the events.

Students are exposed to celebrations vocabulary as they label photos with the names of celebrations.

Answers

1 and 2. Anna's birthday, 3 and 4. Independence Day, 5 and 6. Matt's graduation, 7 and 8. New Year's Eve

2 Read and number the photo captions.

Students learn celebration activities as they match photos of celebrations with their captions.

Answers

top to bottom 2, 5, 4, 1, 6, 3, 7, 8

3 Read and complete the celebration activities.

Students complete the celebration activities mentioned in Activity 2.

Answers

1. resolutions, 2. candles, 3. cap and gown, 4. fireworks, 5. flags, 6. presents, 7. diploma, 8. parade

Wrap-up

Students review the expressions from the vocabulary with a relay race.

- Model the activity by saying one noun from the expressions, for example, *resolutions*.
- Ask a student to come to the board and write the complete expression, *make resolutions.*
- Form two teams and ask them to line up in front of the board. Give the first student in each line a marker.
- Say one of the nouns from the vocabulary. The two students with markers race to write the complete expression on the board. The first team with the correct expression wins a point. Then the students should give their markers to the next person on their teams.
- Say another noun and the next set of students races to finish the expression.
- Continue until you have reviewed all the expressions. Review any expressions that were difficult for students to complete. The team with the most points at the end wins.

 Workbook p. 142, Activities 1 and 2

Teaching Tip

Using Direct Vocabulary Instruction

Try these ways to help students learn vocabulary:

- Explain the new word or phrase using examples, imagery and opposites. Try to tap into students' prior knowledge.
- Have students restate or explain the new vocabulary item in their own words, either verbally or in writing. Encourage students to add their explanations to their vocabulary notebooks.
- Have students create a non-linguistic form of the word, for example, a picture or symbol, and add it to their vocabulary notebooks.
- Have students compare their explanations and images. Encourage them to explain them to each other.

✔ **Homework Check!**

Workbook p. 126, Activities 1 and 2

Answers

1 Look and label.

1a. blow out candles, 1b. open presents, 2a. get a diploma, 2b. wear a cap and gown, 3a. make resolutions, 3b. set off fireworks

2 Look and write the celebration.

1. birthday, 2. graduation, 3. New Year's Eve

Warm-up

Students review celebrations vocabulary by playing *Charades*.

- Choose a celebration from page 14, for example, *graduation*. Act out activities for that celebration: for example, put a cap on your head and accept your diploma, looking proud.

- Elicit the celebration activity: *get a diploma*.

- The first student to guess correctly should come to the front of the class and act out another celebration activity for the class to guess.

- Continue until you have reviewed all the celebrations and celebration activities.

4 🎧³ **Listen and number the celebrations.**

Students number the celebrations in the order they are mentioned in the audio.

Answers

left to right 2, 4, 1, 3

Audio Script

1. Crowd: Five! Four! Three! Two! One! Happy New Year!
2. Every year on the Fourth of July, we celebrate the independence of our country.
3. Teen Boy: We're finally done with high school!
   Man: Congratulations!
   Woman: Good luck at college!
   Teen Boy: Thanks!
4. Family: Happy birthday dear Anna, Happy birthday to you!
   Dad: and many more!

5 **Classify the words.**

Students classify words related to the celebrations.

- Draw students' attention to the **Guess What!** box. Tell them that on New Year's Eve in Denmark, people smash plates against their friends' doors for good luck in the next year.

Answers

Independence Day fireworks, flag, marching band, parade, *birthday* cake, candles, presents, singing, *New Year's Eve* fireworks, *graduation* cap and gown, diploma

6 **Think Fast!** Scramble five celebrations words for a classmate to guess.

Students do a three-minute timed challenge: they choose five celebrations vocabulary words and scramble the letters. A partner guesses the scrambled words.

Extension

Students make their own scrapbook page of celebrations.

- Have students bring in photos of important events and celebrations from their lives, photos from magazines or drawings of images or symbols of life events and celebrations.

- Have them share their photos or drawings in small groups. Monitor and ask questions about the events and how the students celebrated. Provide new words as needed.

- Have students make their own scrapbook pages similar to the one on page 14. Students should label the events. They may add dates, people's names and other important information.

- When students have finished their pages, have them share them with the class. Encourage students to ask each other questions.

Wrap-up

Students consolidate event vocabulary by playing game similar to *Taboo* (or *Hot Seat*).

- Write the name of a celebration or celebration activity on the board.

- Place a chair in front of the class so that the board is behind it. Model by sitting in the chair. Explain that students should describe the event to you, but the words, and all forms of the words, on the board are "taboo," meaning students are not allowed to say them.

- Students form teams and choose a member to come up and sit in the "hot seat." Once the student's back is to the board, write another vocabulary item on the board. The team describes the event to the student in the hot seat without using any forms of the words on the board. Use a stopwatch as a timer. The team who correctly guesses the celebration or celebration activity before time is up wins.

➠ **Workbook p. 126, Activity 3**

 **Grammar**

Objective

Students will be able to use **present continuous** to talk about future plans.

> ✔ **Homework Check!**
> Workbook p. 126, Activity 3
> **Answers**
> **3 Read and complete.**
> 1. watch, 2. athletes, 3. get, 4. picnic, 5. science,
> 6. fireworks

 18

Warm-up

Students review the form of the present continuous with a game.
- Play a game called *What's Happening?* Use the vocabulary in present continuous sentences, having students guess the name of the celebration or event, for example:
  » *I'm walking up an aisle. A lot of people are watching me. I'm receiving my diploma and all the people are clapping. What event am I celebrating?* (graduation)
- Point out or elicit that one usage of the present continuous is to say what is happening at the moment, as with this game.

1 Read quickly and complete.

Students skim a paragraph about Thanksgiving and complete a sentence with information from the paragraph.
- Draw students' attention to the *Guess What!* box. Tell them that pumpkin pie is the most popular pie for Thanksgiving dinners.

Answers

Thanksgiving, Macy's Thanksgiving Day Parade

2 Read and circle the correct option.

Students read the speech bubbles in the comic and choose the correct words to complete each sentence.
- Draw students' attention to the *Present Continuous (Future Meaning)* box and read the information aloud.

Answers

1. next week, 2. are, 3. are

Extension

Students review the present continuous with a guessing game.
- Elicit future events or celebrations. Tell students to choose one and imagine their plans. They should draw a picture to represent their plans.
- Students form pairs and turn back to back. Students take turns asking *yes / no* questions about their partners' pictures, for example, *Are you going to a party? Are you making resolutions?* The student should answer with short answers. Students continue until they guess their partner's plans.

Wrap-up

Students practice the present continuous with a role play.
- Tell students to imagine that they have invited an English-speaking friend to spend a week in their country.
- In groups of three, students discuss and make plans for themselves and their friend for each day of the week. Students should include the following information in their plans: *where they're going, what they're doing, what they're eating, etc.*
- Encourage students to provide as much detail as possible.
- When students have finished, each group presents their plans to the class.

➧ **Workbook p. 127, Activities 1 and 2**

🐝 Teaching Tip

Building Students' Confidence

Confidence is important in learning and using another language. You can build students' confidence in a number of ways:
- Reduce the amount of time you spend talking to the class so that students have more opportunity to interact.
- Avoid asking *yes / no* questions. Ask questions that require a longer response from your students.
- When you correct students, use phrases such as *Why don't you use…* or *Nice try. Now why don't you….*
- Stand back when monitoring and make a list of errors for use in an anonymous feedback session after the activity.
- During fluency practice, don't correct every mistake. Only correct target language when appropriate to the activity.

✔ **Homework Check!**

Workbook p. 127, Activities 1 and 2

Answers

1 Read and match.

1. add –ing to the end of the verb. 2. to talk about future plans.

2 Read and complete the dialogue.

1. taking, 2. What, 3. having, 4. going, 5. meeting, 6. coming

Warm-up

Students practice the present continuous with a game.

- Tell students that they are invited to a Thanksgiving dinner at your house. However, they can't come. Students should think of reasons why they can't come and tell you what they're doing, for example, *Oh, no! I'm going to the dentist that day.*

- Provide some other opening phrases, such as *I'm sorry, I can't make it.* or *That would be nice, but I'm…*

3 🎧⁴ **Listen and mark (✓ or ✗) the plans for the trip.**

Students listen to the family discuss their Thanksgiving trip plans. They should mark the icons that correspond to the family's plans.

Answers

✓ taking the bus, staying with their grandparents, having dinner, watching football, going to the parade
✗ flying, staying in a hotel, going shopping at midnight

Audio Script

MOM STICKMAN: OK, so here are the details about our trip. We're leaving on Wednesday morning—
MAGGIE: How are we going? Are we flying?
MOM: No, we're taking the bus.
MAGGIE: Oh.
OWEN: Are we staying with Grandma and Grandpa or in a hotel?
DAD: We're staying with Grandma and Grandpa. We're watching the parade in the morning—
JO: We're going to the parade?
MOM: Yes!
MOM: We're having dinner with Grandma and Grandpa at 2.
DAD: And then we're watching football on TV.
SARA: Are we going shopping at midnight?
MOM: No. We can go shopping on Friday.

4 🎧⁵ **Listen and circle T (True) or F (False).**

Students do a listening comprehension activity about the family's plans.

Answers

1. F (tomorrow night), 2. F (She is buying a pie.), 3. T, 4. T, 5. T

Audio Script

GRANDPA: When are the kids arriving, Shirley?
GRANDMA: Tomorrow night.
GRANDPA: Is everything ready? Are you making a pie?
GRANDMA: No, not this time. I'm buying a pie at that nice bakery on 43rd Street. And I'm cooking the turkey, the stuffing and the potatoes Thursday morning.
GRANDMA: Don't forget—you're taking the kids to the parade.
GRANDPA: I'm taking them to the parade? Oh, that's right!
GRANDMA: And what are you doing to get ready?
GRANDPA: I'm taking a nap!

5 🎧⁵ **Listen again and unscramble the sentences.**

Students unscramble sentences from the listening.

- Draw students' attention to the **Present Continuous (future meaning)** box and explain the use.

Answers

1. When are the kids coming? 2. I am not making a pie. 3. You are taking the kids to the parade. 4. I am cooking the turkey on Thursday.

6 Think Fast! **In your notebook, write five sentences about Stickman's plans for Thanksgiving.**

Students do a three-minute timed challenge: they write their own sentences about the Stickman family's plans.

Extension

Students compare other celebrations with Thanksgiving.

- Elicit what students know about Thanksgiving.

- Ask students if they know of any events that are similar to Thanksgiving.

- Explain that Thanksgiving is celebrated in the fall, when fruit and grains are ready to harvest. The name *Thanksgiving* means to give thanks for, traditionally, food. Nowadays, people give thanks for the good things in their lives.

- Some other harvest festivals include *Erntedankfest* in Germany, *Kinro Kansha no Hi* in Japan and Canadian Thanksgiving.

- Ask students to research one of these and present their findings to the class.

Wrap-up

Students describe plans for a celebration.

- Ask how Stickman is celebrating Thanksgiving.

- Have students think of an event that they are celebrating soon.

- In pairs or small groups, students take turns describing the planned events. Students try to guess what the events are.

➡ **Workbook pp. 127 and 128, Activities 3 – 5**

⏱ Reading & Listening

Objectives

Students will be able to make a mind map and understand a description of a celebration.

Lesson 5   Student's Book p. 18

✔ **Homework Check!**

Workbook pp. 127 and 128, Activities 3–5

Answers

3 Read and mark (✓).
1. Future, 2. Now, 3. Now, 4. Future, 5. Future

4 Complete using the correct forms of the verbs.
1. 's having / is having, 2. 're going / are going, 3. 'm going / am going, 4. are singing, 5. 's taking / is taking

5 Write the negative forms of the sentences in Activity 4.
1. Julia isn't having a Halloween party next Friday.
2. We aren't going to the baseball game tonight.
3. I'm not going to school tomorrow. 4. Mike and Eva aren't singing a song at the school concert.
5. My aunt isn't taking us to the zoo on Sunday.

Warm-up

Students invent birthday celebrations to generate interest in the reading.

- Ask *Why do we celebrate birthdays?* Elicit answers, for example, *A birthday celebrates the day you were born.* Ask students to say how they celebrate their birthdays.

- Have students form groups and tell them to invent a special celebration for a birthday when they turn a particular age. Tell students to invent a name and some traditions for the celebration, and to say why there should be a special celebration of the age they chose. Encourage them to invent fun or silly celebrations and to note their ideas in their notebooks.

1 Read and circle the correct option.
Students read the text and choose options to complete sentences as a comprehension activity.

Answers

1. Jewish, 2. boy, 3. 12, 4. 18, 5. Muslim, 6. after, 7. eating

2 Read again and complete the mind map in your notebook.
Students use information from the reading to complete a mind map.

- Draw students' attention to the **Be Strategic!** box and read the information aloud.

Extension

Students do some research on "coming-of-age" celebrations.

- Have students do some research on another "coming-of-age" celebration. Here are some questions they should answer:
  - » *At what age is the celebration?*
  - » *Are special clothes worn?*
  - » *Is there special food at the celebration?*
  - » *Is there a different celebration for men and for women?*

- Alternatively, you can assign some celebrations to groups of students and have them research them, for example, a *quinceañera*, confirmation and *seiji shiki*, or you may assign different countries or ethnic groups for students to research.

- Have students present their findings to the class.

Wrap-up

Students perform mind maps of their invented birthday celebrations.

- Have students work in the same groups as they did for the *Warm-up* and take out their notes on their invented birthday celebrations.

- Tell groups to draw a mind map of their invented celebrations using the mind map on page 18 as a model.

- To present their celebrations to the class, groups "perform" their mind maps by assigning group members to represent different nodes on the map. Tell students that they can move around during the presentation to represent more than one point on their mind map.

- Have the class vote on their favorite invented birthday celebration.

⏸▶ **Workbook p. 129, Activity 1**

 Teaching Tip

Managing Fast Finishers
Some students complete activities more quickly than others, so it's a good idea to have a few extra activities on hand. Otherwise these students may become bored and disruptive. One set of activities designed for fast finishers are the *Just for Fun* pages. Students can work on these individually and then check their answers in the back of the Student's Book. The *Just for Fun* activities for this unit are on page 26.

Lesson 6   Student's Book p. 19

✔ **Homework Check!**

Workbook p. 129, Activity 1

Answers

1 Read and complete the facts.

1. First, 2. half, 3. languages, 4. Navajo

Warm-up

Students are introduced to the topic with a memory game.

- Draw students' attention to the photo on page 19. Ask them to say what they see. Students may identify the statue as Buddha. If not, tell them who it is.
- Have students look at the picture for ten seconds and then close their books.
- Have pairs tell each other what they remember in the picture. Ask what the picture shows.

3 🎧⁶ Listen and number.

Students number statements in the order they occur in the listening.

Answers

top to bottom 2, 4, 1, 3

Audio Script

Sunisa here! It's May and next week is a very special holiday for us here in Thailand, and for Buddhists all over the world: Wesak Day! On Wesak, we celebrate the birth, the enlightenment and the death of Buddha. Wesak is a religious celebration, so many Buddhists go to a temple to pray and meditate. They often take flowers and candles with them. At the temple, people give food to the Buddhist monks—men who devote themselves to a simple life (they're easy to identify because they wear robes). At night, everyone walks around the temple three times in a special ceremony. And in general, when we celebrate Wesak, we try to make other people happy, especially people who are poor or sick.

---

4 🎧⁶ Listen again and complete.

Students complete sentences with words from the listening.

Answers

top to bottom candles, happy, world, food, three

5 In your notebook, make a mind map for Wesak Day.

Students organize the information they learned about Wesak Day in a mind map.

Stop and Think! Critical Thinking

What do you know about religious celebrations around the world?

- Draw different religious symbols on the board.
- Elicit or provide the names of the religions that are associated with the symbols.

- Ask students to share any other religions they know. Add their symbols to the board.
- For each religion on the board, ask students to name any celebrations they know of. Have students discuss the celebrations. Elicit what students know about the celebrations.

Wrap-up

Students describe other religious celebrations.

- Divide the class into three or four groups. Assign each group one of the religious celebrations the class listed in the *Stop and Think!* activity. Tell groups to keep their celebration a secret from the other groups.
- Tell the groups to make a a video or short presentation describing the celebration they were assigned. There is just one rule: they have to say a vocabulary word (like *candle, gown, parade, fireworks*) instead of the name of their celebration when they present their podcast to the class.
- Have the other groups guess which celebration each podcast describes and write their answers on a piece of paper.
- After all of the groups have given their information, collect the papers. Groups get a point for each time another group guessed their celebration.

➠ **Workbook p. 129, Activity 2**

Preparing for the Next Lesson

Ask students to watch an introduction to the celebration of the Day of the Dead in Mexico: http:// goo.gl/TPTJbE.

 Teaching Tip

Using Videos in the Classroom

There are a number of reasons to use videos in the classroom. Videos can expose your students to authentic real-world language. Student-made videos, such as news broadcasts, weather reports, documentaries or sitcoms, can be an engaging way to practice language skills.

 **Culture**

Objectives

Students will be able to talk about how the Day of the Dead is celebrated in Mexico.

Lesson 7   Student's Book p. 20

> ✔ **Homework Check!**
>
> Workbook p. 129, Activity 2
>
> **Answers**
>
> **2 Read and complete the mind map in your notebook.**
>
> *Where?* Canada, United States, *Who?* American Indians, *What?* parade, singing, dancing, food, *When?* any time of year, often summer, *How?* wear regular, respectful clothes, have fun

Warm-up

Students activate prior knowledge with a game.

- Tell students that you are going to tell them some facts about Mexico. Tell them that three facts are true, but one is a lie:
  - » *The official name of Mexico is the United Mexican States.*
  - » *Stone tools have been found in Mexico from humans that lived there 23,000 years ago.*
  - » *The most popular sport in Mexico is baseball.* (LIE—soccer)
  - » *The main language spoken in Mexico is Spanish.*
- See if students can guess which one is a lie and correct the statement.
- Tell students they will read some more interesting facts about Mexico.

1 Read the facts about Mexico and underline the one you find the most interesting.

Students read interesting facts about Mexico and choose their favorite.

2 Read and label.

Students read information in a mind map about the Day of the Dead and label the parts of the mind map.

Answers

top to bottom, left to right When? Who? Why? Main Activities, Other Activities

Extension

Students find out more about UNESCO world heritage sites.

- Ask students if they know what the acronym *UNESCO* stands for (United Nations Educational, Scientific and Cultural Organization).
- Have students work in groups to find out more about the 32 world heritage sites in Mexico. You may let the students do all the research or you may assign them a specific site.
- Students should share their findings with the rest of the class.

Wrap-up

Students race to identify the questions that go with each piece of information from the mind map on the Day of the Dead.

- Students form groups of five or six and line up at the board. Each student on each team will take turns going to the board.
- When one student from each team is at the board, read a piece of information from the Day of the Dead mind map (for example, read *people in Mexico: families, schools*).
- The students at the board race to write the mind map heading that corresponds to the information (in the example, *Who?*).
- Watch the students writing on the board and give the point to the team who writes the correct answer first. Continue the game with the rest of the information in the mind map.

▶ **(No homework today.)**

Lesson 8   Student's Book p. 21

Warm-up

Students speculate about the illustration.

- Have students look at the illustration on page 21, covering up the text on the left.

- Have them form pairs and come up with a story about the illustration. Provide some questions to get them started, for example,

  » *What does the picture show?*

  » *Is it a man or woman?*

  » *Why do you think the skeleton is dressed like that?*

- Have pairs share their ideas with the class.

3 Read and answer in your notebook.

Students read about La Catrina and answer comprehension questions about the text.

Answers

1. a skeleton of a woman in an elegant hat and a long formal dress, 2. in 1910, just before the Mexican Revolution, 3. to make fun of wealthy Mexicans who imitated European styles, 4. the Aztec goddess of death and queen of the underworld, 5. Rivera painted a full-length view of La Catrina

Stop and Think! Value

How can holidays bring people together as a community?

- Elicit the holidays and celebrations covered in the unit so far. These include graduation, birthdays, Independence Day, Thanksgiving, Bar and Bat Mitzvahs, Eid al-Fitr, Wesak, the Day of the Dead and any others you have covered.

- Students form pairs and tell each other how the events are celebrated.

- Ask *Which holidays are celebrated mainly with family?* Elicit Thanksgiving and any others you have covered that are appropriate.

- Say *Some holidays and celebrations bring family together. How do the other celebrations bring the people of a community together?* Refer students back to the readings and listening texts.

- Students may talk about how Bar and Bat Mitzvahs are celebrated by the Jewish Community. For Eid al-Fitr and Wesak, people donate to the poor in their communities. For Thanksgiving and Independence Day, people sometimes watch parades together in their neighborhoods. Graduations are celebrated in groups of people from the community who have graduated from high school or college.

Wrap-up

Students use their notes to create a mind map of the reading text.

- Have students take out their notebooks and read the answers to Activity 3.

- Students form small groups and use their notes to create mind maps of the history of La Catrina.

- Have groups present their mind maps to the class and discuss any differences in the way students organized the information.

Teaching Tip

Pre-Reading to Increase Comprehension
Before students read a text, try to take a few minutes to recall and reflect on background knowledge. Follow these steps:

- Begin by reviewing the selection and identifying the main concepts you want to teach. Take into account your students' prior knowledge.

- Decide how you can make these concepts relevant and accessible to all of your students.

- Try using different media, for example, a video, a discussion, visuals or images, or a text you can read aloud.

 **Project**

Objective

Students will be able to make an infographic about a celebration.

Lesson 9 Student's Book pp. 22 and 23

Warm-up

Students guess what certain numbers refer to in order to generate interest.

- Draw a shamrock, like the one on page 23, on the board. Ask students if they know what it is. Elicit or explain that it is a shamrock, which is the symbol of Ireland. Tell students they are going to read about St. Patrick's Day, the celebration of the patron saint of Ireland. Ask them to say what they know about Ireland and St. Patrick's Day.

- Write the following numbers on the board: 387, 461, 1737, 17.

- Tell students that St. Patrick was a real person and the numbers have to do with his life and the holiday.

- Ask students to guess what the numbers refer to.

- Accept any answers. Just let students use their imaginations.

- Tell students they can read the text to find out what the numbers refer to.

Answers

387 the year Patrick was born, *461* the year Patrick died, *1737* the year of the first St. Patrick's day parade, *17* March 17, the day St. Patrick's Day is celebrated

1 Look at the St. Patrick's Day infographic on page 23. Read and match.

Students match words with the sentences that describe them using information from the infographic.

Answers

1. Ireland, 2. shamrock, 3. Murphy, 4. Boston, 5. bagpipes, 6. leprechaun, 7. Australia

2 🎧⁷ Listen and complete the sentences.

Students complete sentences with information from the listening.

Answers

1. Murphy, 2. Sydney, 3. Irish, 4. parade, 5. party

Audio Script

My name is Shaun Murphy. I'm Australian and I live in Sydney, but my family originally immigrated to Australia from Ireland in the 19th century. We still identify with Ireland and its traditions, so we always celebrate St. Patrick's Day. And we aren't the only ones! Here in Sydney, there's a big parade and fireworks. People wear green and decorate things with shamrocks. Our family hangs an Irish flag outside the house. This year we're having a party with Irish music and dancing.

3 Choose and research another celebration's origins and traditions.

Students choose a holiday from those pictured and research the origin of the holiday and how people celebrate it.

Wrap-up

Students review celebrations with a game.

- Students form pairs and choose one of the celebrations from Activity 3.

- They take turns asking and answer *yes / no* questions to try to guess. For example, *Is there an animal? (Yes.) Is it in springtime? (No.) Is it in wintertime? (Yes.) Is it Groundhog Day? (Yes.)* or *Are there candles? (Yes.) Is it a religious holiday? (No.) Is it in the fall? (Yes.) Is it Halloween? (Yes.)*

Warm-up

Students organize a party through a role-play.

- Tell students they are going to organize a St. Patrick's Day party.

- Have them form groups. Elicit some ideas for the party, for example:
  - » *When will it be?*
  - » *What time will it be?*
  - » *Where will it be?*
  - » *Will there be music? If so, what kind?*
  - » *What kind of food will you serve?*
  - » *What kind of games will you play?*
  - » *Who will you invite?*

- Have students decide who will take care of the music, the food, the games, etc., in their groups.

- Have groups tell the class about their parties. Encourage students to use the present continuous to talk about their party plans.

◁ **4 Make an infographic with your findings. Add a party invitation to your infographic.**

Students organize the information they gathered about another holiday or celebration in an infographic. They think about what a party for their holiday would be like and create an invitation for one.

The Digital Touch

To incorporate digital media in the project, suggest one or more of the following:

- Try this online tool for creating infographics: http://www.infogr.am.

- Make your infographic and invitation using free software like Google Docs or Slides.

Note that students should have the option to do a task on paper or digitally.

Wrap-up

Students present research on a celebration.

- Assist students in making notes for a presentation of their research. You may wish to have students work in groups, meeting with other students who chose the same celebration.

- If students are working in groups, help them decide who will present which part.

- Have students practice giving their presentations in groups first.

- Have students present their findings on the celebrations to the class.

⫸ Workbook p. 128, Activities 1 and 2 (Review)

 Teaching Tip

Presenting in the Classroom

Research is a great way for students to learn more about a topic. To get the most out of student research, it should culminate in a communicative activity. In order for a presentation activity to be effective, Students need appropriate support. Here are some tips:

- Consider having students present in groups to take some of the pressure off of individuals.

- Set a reasonable time limit. If you tell students they have to speak for five to ten minutes, they may feel overwhelmed.

- Have students look at the mind maps they made earlier in the unit. Show students how to use the mind map to make and organize notes.

- Give students the chance to practice. Encourage students to practice outside of the classroom, but try to give them at least one chance to do a mock presentation in class.

Review

Objective
Students will be able to consolidate their understanding of the vocabulary and grammar learned in the unit.

Lesson 11 — Student's Book p. 24

✔ **Homework Check!**

Workbook p. 128, Activities 1 and 2

Answers

1 Read the clues and guess the celebration activity.
1. watch a parade, 2. set off fireworks, 3. wear a cap and gown, 4. wave flags

2 Unscramble and answer about you.
1. Is your family going shopping today? 2. Are you going to the dentist tomorrow? 3. Are your friends having a party this weekend? 4. Are you going to school tomorrow?; Answers will vary.

Warm-up
Students list the vocabulary and grammar they have learned in the unit.
- Ask students to think of what they've learned in this unit.
- Elicit and list the grammar and vocabulary on the board. Vocabulary: *birthday, graduation, Independence Day, New Year's Eve; blow out candles, get a diploma, make resolutions, open presents, set off fireworks, watch a parade, wave flags, wear a cap and gown;* Grammar: present continuous (future meaning).

1 Look and label the celebrations.
Students review celebrations vocabulary by labeling photos.

Answers
1. birthday, 2. New Year's Eve, 3. graduation, 4. Independence Day

2 Read and match. Then look and number the scenes.
Students match celebrations collocations. They match illustrations of celebrations activities with the collocations for the activities.

Answers
1. candles, 2. a diploma, 3. fireworks, 4. resolutions, 5. a cap and gown, 6. a parade, 7. flags, 8. presents *top to bottom, left to right* 5, 1, 2, 6, 3, 7, 8, 4

Wrap-up
Students play a game similar to *Jeopardy*.
- Students form teams of four or five.
- Draw the following chart on the board:

Holidays and Celebrations	Celebration Activities	Present Continuous	Culture and Project
10	10	10	10
20	20	20	20
30	30	30	30
40	40	40	40

- Teams take turns choosing an amount and a category, for example, *Holidays and Celebrations for 10.* You then ask them a question and if they answer correctly, that team gets the points assigned to the question.
- Play until all questions have been asked and answered correctly. The team with the most points wins.
- Here are some questions you can ask:

Holidays and Celebrations
100: Everyone celebrates this once a year, no matter your nationality or religion. (birthday)
20: People eat turkey on this holiday in November. (Thanksgiving)
30: This is a religious celebration for Jewish boys. (Bar Mitzvah)
400: This Muslim celebration comes on the first day after Ramadan. (Eid al-Fitr)

Celebration Activities
10: People in the US watch fireworks on this day. (Independence Day)
20: On this day, you receive your diploma. (graduation)
30: On this day, a Jewish girl celebrates her transition into adulthood. (Bat Mitzvah)
40: On this day, Buddhists celebrate the birth, enlightenment and death of Buddha. (Wesak)

Present Continuous
100: What's the present continuous form? *I watch the parade.* (I'm watching the parade.)
20: What's the present continuous form? *He cooks a turkey.* (He's cooking a turkey.)
30: What's the present continuous form? *They visit the temple.* (They are visiting the temple.)
40: What's the present continuous form? *We celebrate St. Patrick's Day.* (We're celebrating St. Patrick's Day.)

Culture and Project
10: What's the smallest breed of dog in the world? (chihuahua)
20: What is the name of a popular symbol for the Day of the Dead? (La Catrina)
30: How many active volcanoes does Mexico have? (11)
40: Where was the first St. Patrick's Day parade? (Boston)

▐▐▶ **(No homework today.)**

Lesson 12 Student's Book p. 25

Warm-up

Students review the vocabulary with a memory game.

- Have pairs make flashcards with celebration activities on them, with each verb on one card and the rest of the phrase on a separate card.

- Students spread the cards face-down on the desk and take turns turning over two at a time, saying the words aloud.

- If a student turns over two "matching" cards, that is, two cards that form a collocation, she keeps that set and takes another turn. If the cards do not match, the student turns the cards face-down again and the other student takes a turn.

- Students play until all the cards have been matched up. The student with the most cards at the end is the winner.

3 Unscramble the sentences.

Students put words in the correct order to form sentences in present continuous.

Answers

1. What are you doing after school? 2. Janice is not going to the party. 3. We are giving Tim a sweater for his birthday. 4. Are you going to the football game tonight? 5. My parents are not having turkey for Thanksgiving.

4 Complete the e-mail using the correct forms of the verbs.

Students complete sentences with verbs in present continuous using cues.

Answers

1. you having, 2. are going, 3. are having, 4. is going, 5. am taking, 6. are not visiting, 7. are taking, 8. are traveling

5 Rewrite the sentences.

Students rewrite sentences in affirmative, negative or interrogative forms.

Answers

1. Are we going to a rock concert tonight? 2. My friend Amy is not / isn't going to the parade. 3. We are / We're setting off fireworks tonight. 4. Paul is / Paul's having a graduation party. 5. Are you going to the party?

Big Question

Students are given the opportunity to revisit the Big Question and reflect on it.

- Ask students to turn to the unit opener on page 13 and think about the question *What do you celebrate?*

- Ask students to think about the discussions they've had about holidays and celebrations, the readings they've read and the infographic they made.

- Students form small groups to discuss the following:

  » *Do you think celebrations are important for families and communities? Why or why not?*

  » *How often do you celebrate with your family? With your friends?*

  » *Which are your favorite celebrations? Why?*

⭐ Scorecard

Hand out (and/or project) a *Scorecard*. Have students fill in their *Scorecards* for this unit.

▸ **Study for the unit test.**

27

2 How are you feeling?

Grammar	Vocabulary

Grammar

***Should*:** You <u>should</u> exercise regularly. You <u>shouldn't</u> drink a lot of soda.

Zero Conditionals: When you <u>reduce</u> your screen time, you <u>have</u> more time for other activities. If you <u>don't sleep</u> enough, you <u>feel</u> terrible.

Vocabulary

First Aid: antiseptic spray, bandages, burn gel, first-aid kit, ice pack, medicine, thermometer

Symptoms and Injuries: bruise, cut, fever, headache, runny nose, sore throat, stomachache, sunburn

Listening

Taking notes to identify main points and supporting examples

Reading

Reading a magazine article

How are you feeling?

In the first lesson, read the unit title aloud and have students look carefully at the unit cover. Encourage them to think about the message in the picture. At the end of the unit, students will discuss the big question: *How are you feeling?*

Teaching Tip

Keeping and Using Vocabulary Notebooks

By now, most of your students are familiar with the idea of a vocabulary notebook, and probably keep one. Here are some tips to make the most of vocabulary notebooks:

Enter only six to ten words per lesson. If students do more than that, it becomes difficult for them to remember and use the vocabulary.

Have students write the entries by hand. Memory retention improves with the physical act of writing down the information.

In addition to definitions, students can also include synonyms, antonyms, collocations or word families.

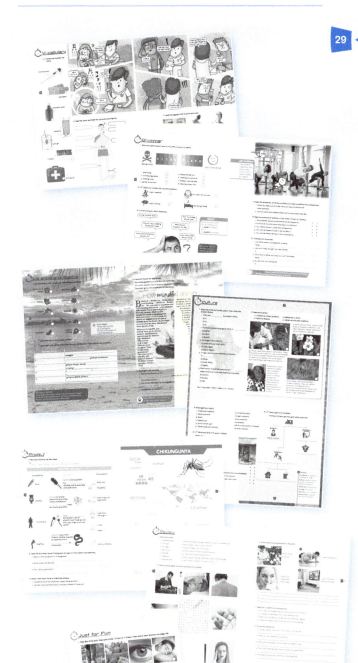

 **Vocabulary**

Objective
Students will be able to use **first aid** and **symptoms and injuries** vocabulary to talk about health.

Lesson 1 Student's Book pp. 28 and 29

Warm-up
Students start thinking about the big question.

- Display photos related to health and medicine: healthy and less healthy food choices, water, bandages, vitamins, etc.
- Elicit how the items are related to health.
- Accept any reasonable answers.

1 ⁸ **Listen and number the items.**
Students are exposed to new vocabulary as they listen to an explanation of what to include in a first-aid kit.

Answers
top to bottom 4, 2, 3, 5, 6, 7, 1

Audio Script
Good afternoon! I'm Dr. Sharon Edwards, and I'm here to help you prepare a first-aid kit. There are many kinds of first-aid kits, and some are very complete. Here are the most important items to include:
You want to have some bandages. Minor injuries are very common and bandages are an excellent way to keep them clean and dry. Before you apply a bandage, clean the area with antiseptic spray. This will help to eliminate dangerous bacteria.
It's a good idea to have a thermometer, and you can also include some medicine.
Get some burn gel, too. We recommend 100% aloe gel.
And don't forget an ice pack. With a quick snap, these become very cold and can treat many minor medical problems.
That's all for now! Watch again next week when I talk about…

2 **Read the comic and label the illnesses and injuries.**
Students are exposed to illnesses and injuries vocabulary in the comic. They label a picture of a man's body with the illnesses and injuries that correspond to each part of the body.

Answers
left fever, sunburn, stomachache, cut
right headache, runny nose, sore throat, bruise

Wrap-up
Students review symptoms and injuries vocabulary by acting out scenes from the comic.

- Students form pairs and act out the scenes from the comic.
- Invite students to suggest items from the first-aid kit that might be useful for the illnesses / symptoms and injuries.

➤ **Workbook p. 130, Activity 1**

🌀 Teaching Tip
Modeling in the Classroom
Teacher modeling is an effective classroom-management technique that not only introduces an activity, but allows students to see an example of what they will be expected to produce. Showing students how to do something ensures better comprehension of directions and reduces anxiety. Here are some specific guidelines for modeling in your classroom:

- Think like a student. When you model, either alone or with a student, think of how they will interpret the activity. It can be highly effective to sit in a desk next to your students or invite a student to the front of the class to help you model the activity.
- Don't overlook the details. If you want your students to use a chart from the Student's Book or their vocabulary notebooks for an activity, point to or show the material. If students need to position their desks, model that as well.
- Observe and verify. Watch closely as your students go through the steps of the activity. Make sure they're on track; if not, stop them and model the activity once more.

Lesson 2   Student's Book pp. 28 and 29

Warm-up

Students review vocabulary with a game.

- Model the activity by acting out one of the illnesses or injuries, for example, *a headache.*
- Other students should guess what the problem is.
- Students form groups and take turns acting out the illnesses and injuries and trying to guess.

3 Look and suggest what to use in each case.

Students review pictures of illnesses and injuries and identify which first-aid items could be used for each.

Answers

left to right (bruise) ice pack, (headache) medicine, (muscle pain) medicine, (sunburn) aloe gel, (sore throat) medicine, (cut) bandage, antiseptic spray, (fever) thermometer

4 Think Fast! Write two examples for each category in your notebook.

Students do a three-minute timed challenge: they classify vocabulary words for symptoms, injuries and first aid.

Possible Answers

Symptoms fever, headache, runny nose, sore throat, stomachache, *Injuries* bruise, cut, sunburn, *First Aid* antiseptic spray, bandages, burn gel, first-aid kit, ice pack, medicine, thermometer

Extension

Students tap into prior knowledge of body parts and use vocabulary in context.

- Have students take out their vocabulary notebooks.
- Have them draw a picture similar to the image on page 28, Activity 2.
- First have them label the body parts they know. Then they add to their picture to represent the injuries and illnesses in the vocabulary.
- Encourage them to list verbs and nouns that go together, for example, *have a headache / stomachache / runny nose / fever / sore throat; have / get a sunburn / bruise / cut.*
- Have students form small groups of three or four to discuss the following questions:

  » *Have you ever injured yourself badly? If so, what happened?*

  » *How often do you get sick? When was the last time you were sick? What was wrong?*

  » *Have you ever broken a bone? If so, which bone and what happened?*

  » *Have you ever had to stay in the hospital? If so, when and why?*

  » *Do you consider yourself healthy? What do you do to stay healthy?*

Wrap-up

Students review vocabulary with a role play.

- Students read the comic again and look over the vocabulary.
- Have students form pairs and make flashcards with the illnesses and injuries on them.
- Model the role play with a more proficient student. Put the flashcards in a pile. Encourage the student to turn one of the cards over.
- Begin by role-playing the doctor, asking, for example, *How are you feeling today, [student's name]?* Elicit an appropriate response, indicating the chosen flashcard.
- Students take turns role-playing doctor and patient using the flashcards.

||||➡ **Workbook p. 130, Activity 2**

Grammar

Objective

Students will be able to use *should* and **zero conditionals** to talk about healthy practices.

Lesson 3   Student's Book p. 30

> ✔ Homework Check!
>
> Workbook p. 130, Activity 2
>
> **Answers**
> **2 Look, read and complete.**
> 1. fever, 2. sunburn, 3. headache, 4. runny nose,
> 5. stomachache, 6. bruise, 7. sore throat

Warm-up

Students review vocabulary with a game.

- Elicit the names of the symptoms and injuries and write them on the board. (Note: Leave these on the board throughout the lesson to use later in the Wrap-up.)

- Hand out pieces of paper. Have each student write one of the symptoms or injuries on a piece of paper.

- Collect the pieces of paper and stick one on each student's back with tape.

- Have students stand up and mingle. They should ask questions about their problem to figure out what their symptoms and injuries are.

1 Rate the health factors. How do they affect a person's health?

Students rank behaviors on a scale from dangerous to very beneficial.

2 🎧⁹ Listen and number the recommendations.

Students are exposed to recommendations with *should* in an audio about healthy practices.

Answers

left to right, top to bottom 1, 3, 4, 2

Audio Script

Hi, I'm Dr. Paul Robinson and I'm here to talk to you about your health. You probably know that you shouldn't eat junk food or smoke cigarettes, and that you should exercise on a regular basis, but *did you know* about these healthy practices?
Number 1. You should always wear a seatbelt when you're in a car. This is important, even for short trips, and even in taxis.
Number 2. Get enough sleep! You should go to bed at the same time every night, and you shouldn't use a phone or tablet before bed. Reducing screen time is very beneficial for your health.
Number 3. When you listen to music, turn down the volume! This is especially important with headphones. You don't want to damage your hearing.
Number 4. Exercise is great for you, but when you ride a bike, you should wear a helmet. Head injuries are very serious, so protect yourself, be safe… and be healthy!

3 Look and answer with a classmate.

Students read questions about healthy and unhealthy practices and answer them with a partner.

- Draw students' attention to the *Should* and *Guess What!* boxes and read the information aloud. Encourage students to use *you should* as they answer the questions.

Extension

Students create and take a survey.

- Have students form pairs. Ask them to list three healthy and three unhealthy habits.

- After students have their lists, come together as a class. Have pairs share their lists, and as a class, decide on five healthy habits and five unhealthy habits.

- Create the first survey item as a class, for example, *How often do you exercise?* Provide a scale for students to include with their surveys:

  1 – very often
  2 – often
  3 – sometimes
  4 – rarely
  5 – never

- Have pairs create a survey that includes the habits and the scale. Pairs should make two copies of their survey.

- Monitor to make sure pairs are creating a survey that can actually be taken.

- When students have finished, collect the surveys and redistribute them.

- Students take the survey and then discuss the results in small groups or as a class.

Wrap-up

Students review grammar and vocabulary with a game.

- Refer to the symptoms and injuries on the board from the *Warm-up*. Have students form pairs and take turns giving advice for how to treat them using *should* and *shouldn't*. The other student should guess which symptom or injury her partner is describing.

▐▶ Workbook p. 131, Activities 1 – 3

✔ **Homework Check!**

Workbook p. 131, Activities 1 – 3

Answers
1 Read and number the suggestions.
left to right, top to bottom 1, 3, 2, 4
2 Complete the sentences using *should* **or** *shouldn't.*
1. shouldn't, 2. should, 3. should, 4. shouldn't
3 Unscramble and answer.
1. Should I eat junk food for lunch? No, you shouldn't. 2. Should I wash my hands before dinner? Yes, you should. 3. Should I brush my teeth at night? Yes, you should.

Warm-up

Students play a game that introduces the concept of zero conditionals.

• Students form groups of four or five.

• Write the following questions on slips of paper:

» *What happens when you stay out in the sun too long?*

» *What happens if you fall out of a tree?*

» *What happens when you eat too much ice cream?*

• Give each group a question. Have students take turns answering the question and forming new questions based on the answer. For example, Student A reads the question *What happens when you stay up late?* Student B answers *You are tired the next day*, and poses the next question, *What happens when you are tired?* Student C answers *You forget to bring your homework*, and so on.

4 Read the sentences. Circle the conditions and then underline the consequences.
Students identify the parts of zero conditional sentences.

• Draw students' attention to the *Zero Conditional* box and explain that we use it to express facts.

Answers
1. When you reduce your screen time, you have more time for other activities. 2. You can avoid many health problems if you eat a balanced diet.

5 Read the examples in Activity 4. Then circle *T* **(True) or** *F* **(False).**
Students confirm their understanding of the zero conditional.

Answers
1. F, 2. T, 3. F, 4. T, 5. T

6 Complete the sentences.
Students write zero conditional sentences using the cues.

Answers
1. When you drink water, your digestion is better.
2. If you don't sleep enough, you feel terrible.
3. When you look at a screen too long, you can't fall asleep. 4. If you exercise regularly, you have more energy.

7 Think Fast! In your notebook, rewrite the sentences in Activity 6. Put the consequence first in each sentence.
Students rewrite zero conditional sentences to place the consequence before the condition.

Answers
1. Your digestion is better when you drink water.
2. You feel terrible if you don't sleep enough.
3. You can't fall asleep when you look at a screen too long.
4. You have more energy if you exercise regularly.

Wrap-up

Students practice writing zero conditional sentences with a game.

• Write a conditional clause on the board, for example, *When it rains…* Invite a student to complete it for example, *I stay home and watch movies.*

• Then write When *If I stay home and watch movies…* and ask another student to complete it.

• Continue in this way with the class. Repeat with other conditional sentences.

➡ **Workbook p. 132, Activities 4 and 5**

Teaching Tip

Using Collaborative Writing in Class
When writing is done collaboratively, it can have many of the same benefits as a speaking activity. Working through ideas is a great way for learners to negotiate meaning. Learners will have to rephrase, clarify, and find new ways to express what they want to say. Working with others can also provide the opportunity for students to work at a higher level than they usually do by cooperating with others who are more proficient.

Listening & Reading

Objectives

Students will be able to take notes to identify main points and supporting examples and read a magazine article.

Lesson 5   Student's Book p. 32

> ✔ **Homework Check!**
>
> Workbook pp. 132, Activities 4 and 5
>
> **Answers**
>
> **4 Read and underline the condition.**
>
> 1. kids eat a lot of junk food, 2. they don't sleep well, 3. I exercise regularly, 4. they study every night
>
> **5 Read and match.**
>
> 1. you eat fewer calories. 2. when you spend too much time online. 3. you make your heart stronger. 4. your body doesn't function well. 5. when you brush them. 6. your body gets the right nutrients.

Warm-up

Students are introduced to the topic with a word game.

- Have students make an acrostic with the word *happy*. Model this by writing an acrostic about what makes you happy on the board:

    » **H**iking with my friends

    » **A**pples

    » **P**etting my cat

    » **P**eaceful moments alone

    » **Y**ellow flowers

- When students have finished, have them share their acrostics. Display them in the classroom.

1 **Look and discuss with a classmate. What makes you happy?**

Students read the list and discuss the things that make them happy.

2 🎧 ¹⁰ **Listen and mark (✓) the topics you hear.**

Students listen to a speaker discuss research findings about what makes people happy and mark the items under Activity 1 that are mentioned in the listening.

Answers

caring about others, exercise, community, pets, positive thinking

Audio Script

March 20th is International Happiness Day. But what makes people happy? It depends on the individual person, but according to scientific research, there *are* some factors that happy people share. At the top of the list is caring about other people—friends, family, even strangers! Just looking at a photo of a friend can make you happy!

Another factor is positive thinking. Examples of positive thinking include optimism, gratitude and kindness. And this one is no surprise: Exercise can also make you happy. When you go to the gym, play sports or take a walk, your body produces *endorphins*—natural substances that make you happy. Pets can make you happy as well. A dog or cat, or even a fish—can brighten your day. Lastly, remember that we humans are social creatures. Community is very important to happiness. Go to a festival, join a club, volunteer! These activities connect us to other people and make us happy!

3 🎧 ¹⁰ **Listen again and add the topics from Activity 2 to the chart. Then complete the examples.**

Students practice taking notes to distinguish main points from supporting examples.

- Draw students' attention to the *Be Strategic!* box and read the information aloud.

- Draw students' attention to the *Guess What!* box. Tell them that according to the United Nation's World Happiness Report, Denmark is the happiest country in the world followed by Norway, Switzerland and the Netherlands.

Answers

1. caring about others: friends, family, 2. positive thinking: optimism, 3. exercise: sports, walk, 4. pets: dog, cat, fish, 5. community: club, volunteering

Wrap-up

Students discuss what is most important to be happy.

- Elicit the things that the listening stated make most people happy: *caring for people, positive thinking, exercise, pets, community.*

- Have students form small groups of three or four to discuss the following questions. *Do the things listed on the board make you happy? Why or why not? What are the three most important things for you to be happy?*

➡ **(No homework today.)**

 Teaching Tip

Managing Fast Finishers

Some students complete activities more quickly than others, so it's a good idea to have a few extra activities on hand. Otherwise these students may become bored and disruptive. One set of activities designed for fast finishers are the *Just for Fun* pages. Students can work on these individually and then check their answers in the back of the Student's Book. The *Just for Fun* activities for this unit are on page 40.

Warm-up

Students do a mindfulness exercise to generate interest.

- Tell students they are going to do a simple exercise called a body scan.

- Have students stand with their eyes closed.

- Tell them to close their eyes and to breathe in and out through their nose. Have them breathe in and out for a few minutes, having them count the breath: *One, two, three in … one, two, three out.*

- Tell them to focus on their attention on their right foot. Tell them to breathe in, imagining they are breathing air in through their foot. After a few breaths, say *Notice how your foot feels.*

- Then tell students to focus their right leg, following the same procedure.

- Continue with the other parts of the body in this order: left foot; left leg; abdomen and belly; upper body, chest, and shoulders; back; right and then left hands and arms; head and face.

- Then tell students to bring their awareness to their whole body. After a few breaths, say, *Notice how it feels now, if it feels any different, if you feel more relaxed.*

- After a few breaths, tell students to open their eyes. Ask for their feedback on the practice: *Did you like it? Will you try it again?*

4 Read and choose the best option.

Students read the article and choose the best summary of the main idea of the text.

Answer

The article explains how to focus on the present moment.

5 Read again and complete.

Students complete sentences about the main points of the article using words from the text.

Answers

1. present moment, 2. Regrets and worries, 3. observe carefully, 4. health, memory

Stop and Think! Critical Thinking

How can being mindful help you to be happy?

- Ask students to think back to how they felt when doing the body scan activity.

- Have students form small groups and brainstorm ways (physical, mental, and any other ways that they think of) mindfulness can help people to be happy.

- Have students come together as a class to share their ideas.

Wrap-up

Students review what they've learned making a podcast.

- Students work in small groups to create a podcast about mindfulness.

- Have groups perform their podcasts for the class. Tell students to feel free to set the tone of their podcast—it can be serious, funny, etc.

▶ Workbook p. 133, Activities 1 – 3

Preparing for the Next Lesson

Ask students to watch an introduction to traditional healers in South Africa: http://goo.gl/LDiAZO or invite them to look around on the web site: http://goo.gl/p0ylnF.

 **Culture**

Objectives

Students will be able to learn about healthcare in Africa.

Lesson 7   Student's Book pp. 34 and 35

> ✔ Homework Check!
>
> Workbook p. 133, Activities 1 – 3
>
> **Answers**
>
> **1 Look and read. What is happening in the picture?**
> The dog has a job. It visits hospital patients.
> **2 Read and answer *T* (True) or *F* (False).**
> 1. T, 2. F, 3. F, 4. T, 5. T, 6. F
> **3 Complete the chart.**
> *Therapy Animals* visit hospitals and nursing homes, help patients to recover from severe injuries, manage grief, overcome anxiety, relax, smile, laugh, reduce blood pressure; dogs, horses, cats, birds, fish; pets with special training
> *Service Animals* live with patients, usually dogs, a range of health conditions, need a lot of training, can go anywhere
> *Both* dogs, training, help humans to be healthy

Warm-up

Students say what they know about Africa to tap into prior knowledge and generate interest.

- Write *Africa* on the board. Ask students to say whether or not the following statements are true or false.

  » *Africa is a country.* (False. It's a continent.)

  » *Africa has the largest desert in the world.* (True. The Sahara is the largest desert.)

  » *Africa has over 2,000 different languages.* (True.)

- Ask students to share what they know about Africa.

1 Read and circle the correct option. Then check the answers below.
Students activate knowledge about Africa by guessing answers to questions and checking their responses.

---

2 Read and number.
Students read an article about healthcare in Africa and match captions to photos.

Answers

top to bottom, left to right 3, 2, 1, 4

3 Read again and match.
Students match the beginnings of sentences about the article with their correct endings.

Answers

1. is very common. 2. have few doctors. 3. is a medicinal plant. 4. plants, animal parts or minerals. 5. modern medicine. 6. are diseases.

Wrap-up

Students think about and discuss the reading text.

- Encourage students to think about their experiences at a doctor's office. Ask *Is it easy to see a doctor? Do you trust your doctors and the medicine they prescribe?*

- Ask *Is it easy for people to see a doctor in some African countries?* Invite students to suggest the advantages and disadvantages of having traditional healers.

- Elicit the people that the text mentions: *doctors, traditional healers, sick patients.* Have students role-play being one of these people. Ask them to explain healthcare in Africa from their point of view. Students should use information from the text.

▐▐▐➤ (No homework today.)

Lesson 8 · Student's Book p. 34 and 35

Warm-up

Students brainstorm possible healthcare problems to generate interest.

- Draw students' attention to the photos in Activity 4.
- Ask *What can you see in the photos?* Elicit any reasonable response, but it should include *a fire, boiling water, people in a village.*
- Ask *What kinds of healthcare problems do you think the people of this village might have?* Elicit any reasonable responses, but it should include *having enough clean drinking water.*

4 🎧" Listen and circle *T* (True) or *F* (False).

Students listen to an audio about a Nigerian healthcare organization and answer true / false comprehension questions.

Answers

1. T, 2. F, 3. T, 4. F, 5. T, 6. F

Audio Script

Blessing Kwomo is a nurse and a healthcare entrepreneur from Nigeria. While working at a hospital, Blessing noticed a problem: many people returned to the hospital. They didn't stay well. Blessing saw that medical treatment was only one part of the path to good health. At just 19 years old, Blessing Kwomo started an organization called the De Rehoboths Therapeutic Studio. This organization provides medical treatment like other clinics, but it also provides health education. For example, they show people how to avoid illnesses at home. Small changes—such as boiling water before drinking it— can prevent serious illnesses. Blessing's organization also provides help for patients to improve their lives. They make repairs to homes. They also teach patients to sew, so that they start their own business and make more money. This money helps the family to buy good food and have a safe, healthy environment.

5 🎧" Listen again and complete.

Students organize information from the listening in a mind map. This information outlines three main ways that Blessing Kwomo's organization helps people.

Answers

Solution 2 health education, boiling drinking water, *Solution 3* help to improve lives, repair homes, teach sewing

Stop and Think! Value

What do you do to stay healthy?

- Write some true / false statements about health on the board, for example:
  - » *You shouldn't eat or drink cold things when you are sick.*
  - » *You can treat your own health problems with information on the Internet.*
  - » *It's OK to share prescription medicine.*
  - » *Natural medicine is always safe for everyone.*
- Elicit whether the statements are true or false. Ask *What do you do to stay healthy? How can it be dangerous if you don't know health information?*
- Students form pairs or small groups to discuss what they do to stay healthy and ways health education can improve wellness.

Wrap-up

Students retell information using a chart.

- Draw students' attention to their completed chart in Activity 5.
- Ask *What is the first solution to the problem?* Elicit *Patients get medical treatment.* If necessary, play the listening again.
- Have students work in pairs to explain the solutions from the listening in their own words.
- Students should produce answers similar to these:
  - » *Patients receive health education.*
  - » *Patients learn that boiling water can help them prevent serious illnesses.*
  - » *Kwomo Blessing's organization provides help for patients.*
  - » *They make repairs to their homes.*
  - » *They teach them how to sew so they can make more money.*

➡ **(No homework today.)**

Teaching Tip

Using Graphics to Support Learning

Graphics and visuals can help students understand and remember difficult concepts. The graphics students create in this unit are a mind map and a fact sheet. However, students have been exposed to many more: charts, graphs, icons, photos and a comic strip. Encourage students to use graphics to assist them when encountering new language.

Objective
Students will be able to make a fact sheet about a disease.

Lesson 9 Student's Book pp. 36 and 37

Warm-up
Students preview vocabulary with a game.

- Play a game called *Call My Bluff* to preview the vocabulary in the Project.
- Give pairs or small groups of students the following vocabulary words and their definitions: *bacteria, virus, fungus, parasite, vaccination.*
- Tell them to invent silly, incorrect definitions for the words. The definitions should sound correct.
- Students take turns saying a word and giving definitions for it. They should choose the definition they like the most for each word.
- Invite volunteers to share their definitions with the class. Then give the correct definitions for each word, writing them on the board:

  » *bacteria: any one of a group of very small living things that often cause disease*
  » *virus: a disease or illness*
  » *fungus: a type of plant that lives on dead things, such as a mushroom*
  » *parasite: an animal or plant that lives on another animal or plant and gets food or protection from it*
  » *vaccination: to put a substance into a person or animal to protect against a particular disease*

1 Read and complete the fact sheet.
Students read the fact sheet and complete it with words from the box.

Answers
top to bottom, left to right infectious, illnesses, cause, transmitted, hands, clean

2 Read the fact sheet about Chikungunya on page 37. Then answer the questions.
Students read a model fact sheet about a virus and use the information to answer questions.

Answers
1. The symptoms are fever, pain in the joints, headache, muscle pain, joint swelling and rash.
2. It is caused by a virus transmitted by mosquitoes.
3. You can prevent it by using mosquito repellant and mosquito nets and emptying water containers.

Wrap-up
Students review infectious diseases with a role play.

- Have students count off, As and Bs. Say that Student A is going to be a journalist and Student B is going to be a doctor of infectious diseases.
- Have Students A meet in groups of three or four to discuss the questions they are going to ask. Have Students B meet in groups to discuss the information and facts they need to know to answer the questions. They should use the chart and fact sheet for support.
- When students are ready, have them pair up, Student A / journalist and Student B / doctor, and perform their role play.

Warm-up

Students analyze a fact sheet to prepare to make their own.

- Draw students' attention to the fact sheet on page 37.

- Ask *What are the sections of the fact sheet?* Elicit *Causes, Symptoms, Prevention.*

- Ask students to show you the title at the top, the different colors of the words and numbers, as well as the larger font.

- Have students discuss in pairs the other features of the fact sheet.

3 Make a fact sheet about an infectious disease.

Students research an infectious disease and make a fact sheet about it, using the model on page 37 and the steps given.

The Digital Touch

To incorporate digital media in the project, suggest one or more of the following:

- Use software like Microsoft Word or Google Docs to create your fact sheet.

- Learn how to make a fact sheet on your PC or Mac: http://goo.gl/h2Lsoq. Students can also use app- or browser-based infographic software such as Canva to create their infographic.

Note that students should have the option to do a task on paper or digitally.

Wrap-up

Students present their infographic about an infectious disease.

- Have students make presentations using their fact sheets.

- Assist students in preparing any notes they need. Explain that notes are just key words and numbers needed to talk about their topic.

- Encourage students to use their fact sheets as a visual aid when presenting.

➠ **Workbook p. 132, Activity 1 (Review)**

 Teaching Tip

Preparing Students for Oral Presentations

You can help students prepare by giving them tips like the following:

- Make eye contact. Tell them it's fine to look at notes, but to make sure to look up and engage their audience.

- Body language is important. Good posture makes you look confident and serious.

- Anticipate difficulties. Students should make sure before presenting that they can pronounce any key or difficult words.

- Speak slowly and clearly. Tell students to speak more slowly than they think they should. When you're nervous, you tend to speed up your speech.

- Practice, practice, practice. Tell students their presentations will go much better and they'll feel more confident if they practice as much as possible.

Make sure to give students time to practice in small groups or in pairs at least once, if not several times, before presenting in class.

Review

Objective

Students will be able to consolidate their understanding of the vocabulary and grammar learned in the unit.

Lesson 11 Student's Book p. 38

➤ 40

✔ **Homework Check!**

Workbook p. 132, Activity 1

Answers

1 Read and correct the sentences.

1. ~~need~~ If you have a cold, your body needs rest.
2. ~~going~~ People shouldn't go to school when they are sick. 3. ~~hands you~~ When you wash your hands, you wash off viruses and bacteria.
4. ~~wanted~~ If people see ads for junk food, they want to buy it.

Warm-up

Students list the vocabulary and grammar they have learned in the unit.

- Ask students to think of what they've learned in this unit.
- Elicit and list the grammar and vocabulary on the board. Vocabulary: illnesses and injuries: *sore throat, runny nose, fever, stomachache, headache, sunburn, bruise, cut*; remedies and first aid items: *thermometer, bandages, antiseptic spray, medicine, burn gel, ice pack, first-aid kit*. Grammar: *should / shouldn't* and zero conditionals.

1 Read and match.

Students review vocabulary by matching vocabulary words with their meanings.

Answers

1. a substance for preventing infection,
2. a substance for skin damage caused by the sun or something hot, 3. a strip of cloth or plastic to cover an injury, 4. a box or bag containing medicines, creams and bandages, 5. a very cold bag to put on an injury, 6. something you take to treat an illness,
7. an instrument for measuring temperature

2 Find and circle eight words for symptoms and injuries.

Students find vocabulary words represented in the photos in the word search.

Answers

left to right, top to bottom stomachache, fever, sunburn, bruise, cut, sore throat, runny nose, headache

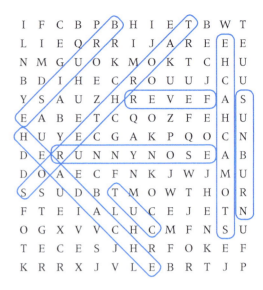

Wrap-up

Students review vocabulary by playing a game like *Pictionary*.

- Students form two teams, each sitting on different sides of the classroom. One member from each team goes to the board.
- Whisper a vocabulary item to the students at the board. The students have one minute to get their teams to guess the vocabulary item by drawing clues on the board. Students cannot use words or letters.
- The first team to guess the word gets a point.
- Continue with new team members until all vocabulary has been reviewed. The team with the most points at the end wins.

➧ **(No homework today.)**

🐝 Teaching Tip

Creating a Student-Centered Classroom

A student-centered classroom is based on collaboration, project-based learning, integration of technology and lots of communication among students. Keep the focus on them with these tips:

- Create ongoing projects. Do this by providing plenty of choices to demonstrate their learning. Be sure to display students' finished projects in your classroom.
- Integrate technology. Encourage students to use digital media to prepare their projects individually or in groups.
- Prioritize fluency as well as accuracy. Consider times when you can focus more on fluency to promote student confidence and involvement.
- Involve students in their own evaluation. A student-centered environment thrives on self-reflection. Encourage students to self-correct and to provide peer feedback when appropriate.

Warm-up

Students review zero conditionals with a card game.

- Prepare a set of cards, one set for every three students, with condition cards and consequence cards. Each condition should correspond to one consequence. Use a different color for conditions and consequences. Here are some possible phrases:

- condition: *stay up late, eat too much candy, exercise regularly, stay in the sun too long, listen to loud music*

- consequence: *feel tired, have a stomachache, have more energy, get a sunburn, get a headache*

- Have students form groups of three and distribute the cards. The consequence cards are dealt out and the condition cards are placed in a pile on the desk.

- The first player turns over the top condition card and makes the beginning of a zero conditional sentence using the phrase on the card. For example, if the phrase is *stay up late*, the student says *If you stay up late…* All the players in the group then look at their consequence cards and find a match to complete the zero conditional sentence.

- The player with a matching card completes the sentence, for example, *If you stay up late, you feel tired the next day.* If everyone agrees that the sentence makes sense, the player with the matching consequence card discards both cards by setting the two cards aside.

- The second player then turns over the next condition card and the game continues.

- The first player to get rid of all her consequence cards is the winner.

3 Write sentences using *should* and *shouldn't*.

Students review *should* and *shouldn't* by writing sentences giving advice about health habits corresponding to the photos.

Answers

1. You shouldn't eat candy for breakfast. 2. You should brush your teeth after every meal. 3. You should exercise regularly. 4. You shouldn't watch TV for six hours every day.

4 Read and underline the consequence.

Students identify the consequence in zero conditional sentences.

Answers

1. you reduce your risk of disease, 2. it's easier to lose weight, 3. you forget about worries and regrets, 4. people are happier

5 Correct the sentences.

Students correct and rewrite zero conditional sentences.

Answers

1. You gain weight when you consume a lot of calories. 2. When you exercise, you burn calories. 3. When you break a bone, it takes six weeks to heal. 4. If you don't drink enough water, you become dehydrated. 5. If you don't wash your hands regularly, you get sick.

Big Question

Students are given the opportunity to revisit the Big Question and reflect on it.

- Ask students to turn to the unit opener on page 28 and think about the question "How are you feeling?"

- Ask students to think about the discussions they've had on health and well-being, the readings they've read and the mind map and fact sheet they made.

- Students form small groups to discuss the following:

  » *How important is good health?*

  » *Is it possible to have a healthy lifestyle in the modern world? Explain.*

  » *There's a saying that goes "Health is wasted on youth." What do you think that means? Do you agree? Why or why not?*

Scorecard

Hand out (and/or project) a *Scorecard*. Have students fill in their *Scorecards* for this unit.

▶ Study for the unit test.

3 How can we save the planet?

Grammar

First Conditional: There <u>will be</u> shortages <u>if</u> we <u>continue</u> to waste water. What <u>will happen</u> if I <u>listen</u> to loud music?

Vocabulary

The Environment: conserve water, plant trees, pollute the environment, recycle, reduce carbon emissions, save electricity, send garbage to landfills, use clean energy, use fossil fuels

Reading

Identifying opinions

Writing

Giving reasons to support your opinions

How can we save the planet?

In the first lesson, read the unit title aloud and have students look carefully at the unit cover. Encourage them to think about the message in the picture. At the end of the unit, students will discuss the big question: *How can we save the planet?*

Teaching Tip

Dealing with Mixed Ability Students

In any class of language students, some students are strong and others need more support. It's important to meet students where they are, giving additional practice to weak students and adjusting activities to be more challenging at times for stronger students. However, few students are always strong in every area all the time. Likewise, weak students may have strengths they aren't aware of. Using the Stopwatch *Scorecards* at the end of every unit can help them to discriminate between these areas and grow in their language abilities.

Vocabulary

Objective
Students will be able to use **the environment** vocabulary to talk about environmental issues.

Lesson 1 Student's Book pp. 42 and 43

Warm-up
Students discuss their opinions on the environment to generate interest and access prior knowledge.

- Ask *What environmental problems have you heard about in the news lately?* Elicit some responses.
- Ask *What is the most serious problem facing the planet right now?*

- Students form small groups of three or four and do a round-robin, where each student expresses his opinion. Only after all opinions are expressed can students respond.
- Come together as a class and have some students share their thoughts and ideas.

1 Read and circle the correct option.
Students read the *Create Awareness* flyer and use the information to choose the correct option for each photo.

Answers
1. pollute the environment, 2. use fossil fuels, 3. recycle, 4. use clean energy

2 Complete the phrases and answer. Which actions help the environment?
Students identify and complete vocabulary collocations using the words in blue in the text.

Answers
1. plant, 2. save, 3. pollute, 4. reduce, 5. water, 6. landfills, 7. energy, 8. fuels; *actions that help the environment* 1, 2, 4, 5, 7

3 Match the verbs with the definitions.
Students determine the meaning of vocabulary through context and identify the definition of each verb.

Answers
1. to protect a natural resource, 2. to collect or avoid using something, 3. to transform objects into new things, 4. to introduce garbage and chemicals to a place, 5. to put something in the ground to grow

Wrap-up
Students create flashcards and play a *Memory* matching game to review vocabulary.

- Students form pairs.
- Have pairs take out a sheet of paper and cut it into eighteen pieces.
- Have students write part of a vocabulary phrase on one of the pieces, and the rest of the phrase on another piece. For *recycle*, have them draw a recycling symbol on the second piece. Students should write lightly in pencil so that the words are not visible through the paper.
- Ask students to place all the cards on the desk, face-down.
- One student turns over two cards. If the pieces of paper match, for example, *plant trees*, the student says the collocation, keeps the pair and plays again. If they don't match, the student should place them face-down in the same spot.
- Students play until all pairs are matched up. The student with the most pairs wins. Have students keep their flashcards to practice again in the next lesson.

 Workbook p. 134, Activity 1

Teaching Tip
Facilitating Discussions
Discussions are useful for many reasons: They encourage students to consider other opinions and points of view, they foster understanding and empathy, and they promote higher-order thinking, among others.
Here are some tips for successful discussions:

- Rearrange desks if possible. If students can't see each other, the exchange will be limited.
- Ask questions that have multiple answers.
- Encourage students to justify their responses and opinions.
- Give students enough time to think about their responses before expecting them to speak.

✔ Homework Check!

Workbook p. 134, Activity 1

Answers
1 Look and complete the sentences.
1. saves, 2. planting, 3. 're / are using,
4. 're / are using, 5. send, 6. conserve, 7. Reducing

Warm-up

Students review vocabulary with their game pieces and play a game of *Go Fish!*

- Pairs take out their vocabulary game pieces from the *Wrap-up* activity in the previous lesson.

- Students form groups of four, made up of two pairs. One student shuffles the pieces of paper and deals the four to each group member. The rest are spread out face-down in the middle of the desk. This is the "lake" that students will "fish" from.

- The first player should ask the student to her left for a vocabulary word or phrase that corresponds to one in her hand. For example, if she has *trees*, she asks *Do you have plant?* If the other student has the corresponding card, he gives it to her, and she may play again with the next student. If he doesn't, he says *Go fish!* and she draws a card from the lake. If it is a match, she continues. If not, the next student plays.

- Students continue until all cards are matched up, or as time permits. The student with the most pairs after all cards are matched up wins. Have students keep their flashcards to practice again in Lesson 4.

4 🎧¹² **Listen and number the suggestions.**

Students listen to the advice and number the icons in the order they hear them.

- Draw students' attention to the *Guess What!* box. Tell them that fossil fuels like oil and gas come from plants that were alive millions of years ago!

Answers

3, 1, 4, 2

Audio Script

There are many things you can do to protect the environment and reduce carbon emissions. Here are a few practical suggestions:
1. Wear a sweater! On cold days, your house shouldn't be really warm. That uses a lot of energy. It's better to set the temperature to 18 degrees, not 20 degrees.
2. Read a book! Books don't require electricity like many other forms of entertainment.
3. Eat less meat. Hamburgers are delicious, but cows need a lot of water and *their* emissions pollute the environment.
And the last suggestion is a lot of fun if you have the money:
4. Buy a new car! New cars are more efficient. They use less gasoline than older cars—and sometimes *no* gasoline.
Remember, we only have one Earth, so we have to take care of it!

5 **Think Fast! Read and mark (✓) about you. Then calculate your score.**

Students do a three-minute timed challenge: they answer a quiz about their own behaviors related to the environment and score their answers.

Extension

Students conduct research on an environmental topic using printouts of news articles.

- Students form groups of three.

- Assign each group one environmental topic. Give groups printouts of news articles about their topic.

- Give students time to read their news article and list three facts from it.

- Have students present their research to the class. Encourage other students to ask questions.

Wrap-up

Students discuss the results of a quiz.

- Draw students' attention to the quiz they took in Activity 5.

- Students form small groups of three or four. They compare the results of the quiz.

- Encourage them to discuss ways they could care for the environment more.

➤ **Workbook p. 134, Activity 2**

 **Grammar**

Objective

Students will be able to use **first conditional** to talk about environmental problems and solutions.

 Lesson 3 Student's Book p. 44 and 45

> ✔ **Homework Check!**
>
> Workbook p. 134, Activity 2
>
> **Answers**
> **2 Correct the spelling errors.**
> 1. electricity, 2. clean energy, 3. garbage,
> 4. landfills, 5. pollution, 6. environment

Warm-up

> **46**

Students review environment vocabulary with a word unscrambling activity.

- Write individual words from the environment vocabulary on the board with the letters scrambled, for example, *ldslnaifl (landfills).*
- Give students two minutes to unscramble and write as many words as possible.
- Check the answers together as a class. Elicit the correct spelling of each word and the phrase it is a part of: *L-A-N-D-F-I-L-L-S; send garbage to landfills.*

1 Look at the picture and mark (✓) the actions that help the environment and (✗) actions that pollute the environment.

In preparation for the reading, students identify actions that are helpful or harmful to the environment.

Answers

not cleaning up after a pet ✗, cycling ✓, picking up litter ✓, driving a car ✗, listening to loud music ✗, taking a short shower ✓, using solar energy ✓, flying in a plane ✗, wasting water ✗, wasting electricity ✗, polluting the environment ✗

2 Read the *Ask Miss Eco* column and underline the four environmental problems.

Students read the column and identify the problems.

Answers

1. dog poop, 2. loud music / noise pollution, 3. light pollution, 4. air pollution

3 Read the magazine article again and complete the sentences.

Students find the first conditional sentences in the text and use words from the column to complete them.

Answers

1. the city will be much cleaner, 2. if I listen to loud music, 3. If we use lights everywhere, 4. If I take a shower every day, 5. there will be fewer cars in the streets and less pollution in the air

Extension

Students play a game of *Snakes and Ladders* to practice the first conditional.

- Create a board game with a path of 35 numbered blocks. Connect some blocks with snakes or ladders. Ladders advance the student past future squares. Snakes cause the player to return to earlier squares.
- Write *if*-clauses and consequences in the boxes. Leave the boxes with the snake heads and the bottom of the ladders blank. Make a copy of the game board for each group.
- Students form small groups. Give each group a game board and a die. Tell students to find a place marker like an eraser or paper clip.
- Each student takes a turn rolling the die and moving his marker forward the number of spaces shown on the die. The student uses the clause or phrase to say a first conditional statement.
- The student who makes it to the last square first wins.

Wrap-up

Students review the first conditional with a game.

- Write the following sentence on the board: [Your name] *for president!*
- Say *I'm running for president. I want you to vote for me! If you vote for me, I'll …* Complete the sentence with something that will appeal to your students, for example, *do away with tests!* Tell them this is your "election promise."
- Tell students that they are all running for president, too. Students think of their election promises and write them on a piece of paper.
- Have each student stand up in front of the class and say her election promise.
- Students vote for the best candidate.

⮕ **Workbook p. 135, Activities 1 and 2**

Teaching Tip

Managing Your Classroom Effectively

Keeping your lessons flowing smoothly is necessary for your students' learning. Here are some tips:

- Speak only when students are quiet and ready to listen. Even if you have to wait longer than you think, sometimes saying nothing gets more attention than anything you might say.
- Use hand signals and other non-verbal communication. Holding one hand in the air or flicking the lights off and on once is sure to get your students' attention.
- Always have a well-designed and engaging lesson. Make sure you have plenty of activities to fill class time. It's better to run out of time than to run short on a lesson.

✔ Homework Check!

Workbook p. 135, Activities 1 and 2

Answers

1 Read and underline the consequence.

1. we will have enough water in the future,
2. We will pollute the environment more,
3. we will bother our neighbors, 4. We will make our cities nicer, 5. we will send less garbage to landfills

2 Complete using the correct form of the verb.

1. listen, 2. will not / won't be able, 3. will use, 4. share, 5. will make

Warm-up

Students practice the first conditional with a round-robin.

- Say an *if*-clause in the present tense, for example, *If we take long showers every day…* and elicit the consequence from a student, for example, *we will use a lot a water.*

- The next student makes an *if*-clause with the consequence, for example, *If we use a lot of water…* and the next student completes it with a consequence, for example, *the world will not have enough.*

- Repeat several times.

4 🎧 ¹³ **Listen to the interview and mark (✓) the topics that the people talk about.**

Students identify and mark the topics in the audio.

Answers

washing the dishes, washing clothes, consuming energy, using electricity at home

Audio Script

REPORTER: I'm with Margaret Smith, an expert in urban environments. Margaret, you say that we are very wasteful. What does it mean? Can you tell us some more?

MARGARET: Yes, of course. First of all we waste a lot of electricity. I think that we can save a lot of electricity at home by doing a few simple things. For example, if we change standard lightbulbs for compact fluorescent lightbulbs, we will use 75% less energy.

REPORTER: Wow. That's a lot!

MARGARET: It is! And of course, you should turn off the lights if you don't need them!

REPORTER: What about water? Some people say you use less water if you wash dishes by hand. Is that the case?

MARGARET: No, it's not. An automatic dishwasher uses about 22.7 liters of water less than washing by hand.

REPORTER: Really! What about using washing machines? If we use cold water, will the clothes be as clean as with hot water?

MARGARET: Sure! If we use cold water, the clothes will be just as clean as with hot water. It is a myth that stains disappear only with hot water.

REPORTER: What's the biggest user of energy in our homes?

MARGARET: Well, believe it or not, it's heating. This accounts for about 30% of the energy we use in a house. We will save energy and money if we use less heating at home. Also, every time we leave the refrigerator door open, up to one third of the cold air escapes.

REPORTER: Well, it's clear things will only get better if we take steps to protect our environment.

5 🎧 ¹³ **Listen again and mark T (True) or F (False).**

Students listen again for detail and mark whether each statement is true or false according to the interview.

Answers

1. F (We will save 75% more energy.), 2. F (Washing dishes by hand uses more water than a dishwasher.) 3. F (Using cold water is just as good as using hot water.), 4. F (Heating is the biggest user of energy at home.), 5. T

6 Think Fast! Read the conditions and consequences. Then connect the sentences using the first conditional.

Students do a five-minute timed challenge: they combine the phrases in the diagram into first conditional sentences.

Answers

If I don't turn off the lights, I'll waste more electricity. If I waste more electricity, the electric bill will be more expensive. If the electric bill is more expensive, I'll spend more money. If I spend more money, I won't have money to go out. If I don't have money to go out, I'll stay home. If I stay home, I'll use more electricity.

Wrap-up

Students practice the first conditional with flashcards.

- Have pairs take out their flashcards from the Lesson 1 *Wrap-up* activity.

- Pairs match up each verb with the word or phrase that completes the vocabulary item.

- One student makes an *if*-clause, for example, *If we take short showers…* The other student finishes it with one of the vocabulary items, for example, *… we will conserve water.*

- Then students switch.

- Students continue until all the vocabulary items have been used.

▶ **Workbook p. 135, Activities 3 and 4**

Reading & Writing

Objective
Students will be able to identify opinions and give reasons to support their opinions.

Lesson 5   Student's Book pp. 46 and 47

✔ **Homework Check!**

Workbook p. 135, Activities 3 and 4

Answers

3 Read and switch the order of the condition and the consequence.
1. We will save electricity if we use cold water to wash clothes. 2. We will change the Earth's climate if we don't use clean energy. 3. If the Earth's climate changes, many animals will go extinct.
4 Look and write the questions. Then answer.
1. Where will people live if cities disappear underwater? 2. What will happen if many animals go extinct? 3. How will we grow food if bees go extinct? Answers will vary.

Warm-up
Students express and defend their opinions with a kinesthetic activity called *Four Corners*.

- Write the following words and phrases in big, easy-to-see letters on separate sheets of paper: *Strongly Agree, Agree, Disagree, Strongly Disagree*. Place these signs, one in each of the four corners of your classroom.

- Say a statement, for example, *People don't have to clean up after their dogs*. Students go to the corner that best matches their opinion.

- The students in the same corner discuss why they chose that opinion. After a few minutes, have each group report to the class.

- Read another statement and follow the same procedure. Here are some examples of statements:

  » *Recycling should be mandatory.*

  » *Bikes should not be allowed in cities.*

  » *The government should promote vegetarianism.*

  » *Gasoline prices should be higher so people will drive less.*

1 Look and write the headings.
Students look at the photos and label them with the headings provided.

Answers

top to bottom Wearing Fur Coats, Keeping Animals in Zoos, Being Vegetarian

---

2 Read the statements. Write F (For) or A (Against).
Students read the statements for each topic and mark which ones are for and which are against the position indicated in the heading.

Answers

top to bottom F, A, F, A, F, A

---

3 Read the statements on page 46 again. Which arguments do you agree with? Underline the arguments that sound more convincing.
Students reread the statements from Activity 2 and choose the ones they agree with and the ones that are most persuasive.

Wrap-up
Students review vocabulary by writing short stories.

- Draw students' attention to the words in the Glossary on page 47.

- Students form pairs or groups of three.

- Tell students to write a short story using the five words. The story can be about the planet, but it doesn't have to be.

- Have students share their stories with the class.

▶ Workbook p. 137, Activities 1 and 2

🐝 Teaching Tip
Managing Fast Finishers
Some students complete activities more quickly than others, so it's a good idea to have a few extra activities on hand, otherwise these students may become bored and disruptive. One set of activities designed for fast finishers are the *Just for Fun* pages. Students can work on these individually and then check their answers in the back of the Student's Book. The *Just for Fun* activities for this unit are on page 54.

▶ 48

✔ **Homework Check!**

Workbook p. 137, Activities 1 and 2

Answers

1 Read quickly and answer. What requires the most water?

a

2 Read and underline the information. Write the amount.

1. 2 liters, 2. 167 liters, 3. 3,496 liters, 4. 15,400 liters, 5. 30%

Warm-up

Students determine reasons for opinions.

• Have students reread the opinions in Activity 1.

• Elicit or provide the three questions that one would use to ask someone's opinion on the topics in Activity 1 and write them on the board:

» *How do you feel about wearing fur?*

» *What's your opinion on zoos?*

» *What do you think about eating meat / being a vegetarian?*

• Students form pairs.

• Tell students to find the two opinions that answer each question.

• Then ask *What reasons do the people give for their opinions? Find the reasons in the text. Imagine that you have that opinion. Restate the opinion in your own words.*

• Pairs identify the reasons and take turns restating them in their own words. Challenge students to restate each opinion and reason in one sentence.

• Some example answers are:

» *I'm not against wearing fur because we use animal skin for other things.*

» *I think zoos are cruel because they keep animals locked away in an unnatural environment.*

» *I think it's a good idea to be vegetarian because it's wrong to kill animals and harm the environment, and because it's healthier.*

4 Complete the opinion expressions.

Students find the opinion expressions in the text and complete them with words from the statements.

Answers

1. many reasons, 2. nothing wrong, 3. good for, 4. against, 5. not against, 6. don't agree

5 Choose a topic from page 46. Write a sentence to state your opinions using an expression from Activity 4.

Students practice giving their opinion using opinion expressions. Then they read the *Be Strategic!* tip.

6 Add two or three reasons to support your opinion.

Using the statements from Activity 2 as a model, students add two or three reasons to the opinion statement they wrote in Activity 5.

Stop and Think! Critical Thinking

How can you develop an informed opinion about something?

• Ask students to discuss this question. Then discuss as the class. Elicit characteristics of a reliable source and write them on the board.

Extension

Students learn more about vegetarianism.

• Ask *Do you know what the difference is between a vegetarian and a vegan?* Elicit *Both vegetarians and vegans don't eat any meat (beef, pork), poultry (chicken, turkey, duck) or seafood (fish, shrimp, clams). While vegetarians may eat eggs and drink milk, vegans don't eat any animal products, including honey.*

• Discuss the following questions as a class:

» *Do you know any vegetarians or vegans?*

» *What are some reasons for becoming a vegetarian?*

» *What are the health benefits of a vegetarian diet? Are there any health problems?*

• Students form small groups of three or four. Write the following questions on the board for them to discuss:

» *How would your friends react if you became a vegan?*

» *What if you wanted to become a vegan and your parents were against it?*

» *If you were a vegetarian, would you work in a restaurant that serves meat?*

» *How do you feel about other animal products, for example, leather, wool and silk?*

Wrap-up

Students express and defend their opinions with the *Four Corners* from the previous lesson.

• Using the signs and procedure from the Warm-up activity in Lesson 5, play *Four Corners* with the statements from Activity 4.

• Students discuss why they chose that opinion and share their thoughts with the class.

⬛➡ **Workbook p. 137, Activity 3**

Preparing for the Next Lesson

Ask students to watch a video about electricity and green energy in Japan: http://goo.gl/61Em00.

 **Culture**

Objectives
Students will be able to talk about nuclear energy in Japan.

Lesson 7   Student's Book pp. 48 and 49

> ✔ Homework Check!
>
> Workbook pp. 137, Activity 3
>
> **Answers**
> **3 Decode the water footprint for each item (1=a, 2=b, etc.).**
> 1. 1,786, 2. 822, 3. 18,885

▶ 50 **Warm-up**

Students play a game called *Two Truths and a Lie* to generate interest.
- Tell students some facts about Japan. Say three things that are true and one that is a lie, for example:
  - » *Almost 130 million people live in Japan.*
  - » *In 2011, a volcano erupted in Japan.*
    (LIE—earthquake)
  - » *There are over 50 nuclear reactors in Japan.*
  - » *People in Japan don't want to use nuclear energy.*
- Students guess which statement is a lie.
- Tell students they will read an article to find out which one is the lie.

1 Read and number the photos.
Students match photos with information about Japan.

Answers
top to bottom, left to right 4, 3, 1, 2

2 Read the article. Is nuclear energy a good option? Why or why not?
Students read the article about nuclear energy in Japan and form an opinion on the topic.

Wrap-up
Students review a text by explaining vocabulary.
- Have students take out a piece of paper and tear it into six pieces.
- Draw students' attention to the article in Activity 2. Students choose six words that they think are challenging. This can include words from the glossary. They write these words on the six pieces of paper.
- Students form pairs.
- Students take turns describing the word to their partner for him or her to guess the word.

▶ **(No homework today.)**

 Teaching Tip

Making the Most of Reading Activities
There are many reasons why reading is an important strategy for your students. Here are a few tips for getting the most out of the activities that come before, during and after a reading:
- Preview key words and terms beforehand. Something as simple as writing the key words on the board and having students underline them in the reading helps students to focus their attention on important words and ideas.
- Teach students how to decipher meaning from context. As a follow-up activity, have students explain what the key words mean in the context of the reading, using the text to support their answers. Encourage them to use this strategy with other new words they come across.
- Have students quiz each other about the reading. After reading, have students come up with several questions and then ask each other to answer them, using evidence from the text.
- To promote fluency, find a way to turn the topic of the reading into a discussion, debate or role play.

Warm-up

Students play a game to review information about Japan from the previous lesson.

- Students form pairs. One student closes her book and the other student names something from page 48: *umi budo*. The other students says what it refers to: a *dish from Okinawa*.
- Students take turns quizzing each other.

3 🎧¹⁴ **Listen and answer. Why is the town of Kamikatsu a special place?**

Students listen to a description of how garbage is handled in a Japanese town and discuss what is special about the town.

Audio Script

Kamikatsu is a small town in southern Japan. Only about 2,000 people live there. But it's a special place because they produce very little garbage. And by the year 2020, they hope to produce no garbage. But how do they do it? They are very responsible. The town doesn't have a garbage truck. People must collect their own garbage, wash it and take it to a collection center. They recycle most of the garbage. They don't just separate their glass, paper, plastic and metal; they have 34 different categories for recycling. They separate magazines from newspapers, and soda cans from spray cans. They also have a factory where they make new clothes using the material from old clothes. In Kamikatsu, almost nothing goes to waste!

4 🎧¹⁴ **Listen again and circle T (True) or F (False).**

Students listen to the audio for detail and determine whether statements about the information in the listening are true or false.

Answers

1. F (It is in southern Japan.), 2. T, 3. T, 4. T, 5. F (There are 34 recycling categories.), 6. F (They make new clothes using material from old clothes.)

Stop and Think! Value

How can you create less garbage?

- Ask students to think about their daily routine with the following questions:
  - » *Do you drink canned or bottled beverages? If so, how often?*
  - » *How often do you eat fast food or take-out food?*
  - » *How often do you bring your own bag when you shop?*
  - » *Do you have any many magazines subscriptions? If so, how many?*
  - » *How many bags of trash do you or your family fill every week?*
  - » *How often do you go shopping for new clothes?*

- Tell students to think about these questions and to discuss them in small groups, focusing on the amount of garbage created by different habits and activities.
- Then ask *How can you create less garbage?*
- Students discuss in small groups.
- Come together as a class, having some students share their thoughts and ideas.

Extension

Students debate the pros and cons of nuclear energy.

- Divide the class into two groups. One group is pro nuclear power; the other group is against it.
- Here are some sample questions they can research:
  - » *Is nuclear power safe?*
  - » *Can nuclear energy be good for the environment?*
  - » *Are there safe ways to deal with nuclear waste?*
  - » *Can nuclear power coexist with renewable energy sources?*
  - » *What is the general public opinion on nuclear power?*
- When students are ready to debate, arrange the room so that there are two rows of chairs facing each other. The students who are for nuclear power sit on one side and the students who are against it sit on the other.
- Toss a ball to a student on the "against" side. Begin with a statement that is in favor of nuclear power, such as *Nuclear power is good for the environment.*
- The student with the ball responds to your statement. Then that student tosses the ball to a student who is for nuclear power, and that student responds.
- The ball is tossed back and forth until the debate is finished or as time permits.

Wrap-up

Students retell the audio in their own words.

- Draw students' attention to Activity 4. Ask *Which sentences are false?* Elicit *1, 5* and *6*.
- Students form pairs and retell the audio in their own words, correcting the statements from Activity 4.

▶ **(No homework today.)**

Project

Objectives
Students will be able to make a mini documentary.

Lesson 9   Student's Book p. 50

Warm-up
Students guess the meaning of vocabulary with a game called *Call My Bluff*.

- Have students close their books.

- Write and number the vocabulary items from the Track 15 on the board: *1. litter, 2. trash, 3. dumpster, 4. wrappers, 5. infuriating.*

- Students count off to form five groups.

- Assign one word to each group. Provide each group the definition for their vocabulary item from the glossary on page 50.

- Tell students that they should think of another definition, one that might fool their classmates.

- Have groups read both definitions aloud. The other students try to call their bluff and say which is the correct definition.

1 Look and match the symbols with the slogans.
Students find the symbol that goes with each slogan. They draw lines from the slogans to the symbols. (The boxes are for the next activity.)

Answers
slogans left to right, top to bottom person putting trash in trash can, wind turbine, recycling symbol, water drop, lightbulb

2 🎧¹⁵ Listen to the script and mark (✓) the topics.
Students listen and mark the boxes next to the symbols in Activity 1 which correspond to the topics in the listening.

Answers
recycling, not littering

Audio Script
I think we live in a really clean area, and people in our community care about the environment. A lot of people sort their trash and take their recycling to the special dumpster at the park. You can recycle paper, plastic, glass and metal. The dumpster is always full. But we can improve things. Garbage trucks should collect the recycling, so that more people participate. Also, we should use fewer containers! Recycling is good, but people should reuse their containers. We also have a problem in the community. Many people throw trash out of their cars. In some places, the ground is covered in bottles and bags and wrappers. It's very sad. If people continue littering like this, no one will want to visit our area and it will even harm the wildlife. But if we work together, we can clean it up and keep it nice.

3 🎧¹⁵ Number the missing fragments of each script. Then listen again and check.
Students write the numbers of the missing sections of text to complete the scripts.

- Draw students' attention to the **Guess What!** box. Tell them that you don't need to be an important political figure to change your community. There are thousands—maybe millions—of teen activists in the world. They see a problem and look for a way to solve it.

Answers
8, 2, 6, 4, 5, 3, 7, 1

Wrap-up
Students come up with an environmental slogan.

- Draw students' attention to the slogans in Activity 1. Ask *What is the topic of each slogan?*

- Have students form small groups to create their own slogans. Encourage students to think about their communities and which activities help or hurt the environment, and then to think of a slogan that could promote helpful activities or discourage harmful ones.

🐝 Teaching Tip
Checking for Comprehension
Here are some tips to confirm students' understanding:

- Do a *Think-Pair-Share* activity, in which students think about a question, that is related to the lesson, discuss it in pairs and share their answer with the class. For example, ask *Which four problems does the speaker mention?*

- Use response cards. Instead of calling on one or two students, have every student write the answer on a small card and hold it up.

- Have students use hand signals to indicate their level of understanding. Students can hold up five fingers to show maximum understanding to one finger for minimal understanding.

- Ask students to summarize or paraphrase. This can be orally or in writing, or even through drawing.

- Use the *3-2-1* method. Students consider what they've learned by responding to this prompt: *What are 3 things I've learned from the lesson? What are 2 things I want to know more about? What is 1 thing I didn't understand very well?*

Warm-up

Students brainstorm environmental issues.

- Ask *What are some of the environmental issues we've covered in this unit?* Write the students' answers on the board.

- Students form pairs.

- Say *Think about your community and its environmental problems.* Ask *What possible solutions or alternatives can you suggest?* Give students time to answer in pairs.

- Have pairs share their ideas with the class.

◁ **Make a mini documentary about your community.**
Following the steps given, students make a mini documentary about an environmental issue in their community.

The Digital Touch

To incorporate digital media in the project, suggest the following:

- Use a phone or tablet to record and edit your project with an app like Andromedia Video Editor (Android, https://goo.gl/sXgsfJ) or iMotion (Apple, https://goo.gl/h2HMpn).

Note that students should have the option to do a task on paper or digitally.

Extension

Students hold a "film festival."

- Ask *What makes a good documentary?* Elicit or provide the following criteria: *useful information, a clear message, interesting interviews*, etc.

- Tell students that they will vote on the best documentary. Decide if there will be first prize, second prize and third prize or simply one winner.

- Have students screen their films in class. Encourage students in the audience to use the criteria above as the basis for their decisions.

Wrap-up

Students discuss what they learned from making their mini documentaries.

- Write the following questions on the board:

  » *How did you decide what you would film?*

  » *Were the people you filmed eager to work with you or not?*

  » *What did you learn from making your mini documentary?*

  » *Do you think your mini documentary will have an impact on your community? Explain.*

- Students form small groups with one student representing each documentary to discuss the questions.

▐▐▐▶ **Workbook p. 136, Activities 1 and 2 (Review)**   **53** ◀

 **Review**

Objective
Students will be able to consolidate their understanding of the vocabulary and grammar learned in the unit.

Lesson 11   Student's Book p. 52

✔ **Homework Check!**

Workbook p. 136, Activities 1 and 2

Answers

1 Read and correct the sentences.
1. ~~doesn't~~ If people <u>don't</u> conserve water, there won't be enough water in the future. 2. ~~water we~~ If there isn't enough water, we won't be able to grow food. 3. ~~doesn't~~ We will change the climate if we <u>don't</u> reduce carbon emissions.

2 Answer about you.
Answers will vary.

Warm-up
Students review vocabulary with a game.

• Write the mirror-image of the environment vocabulary items on the board, for example:

• Students form pairs.

• Pairs race to identify and correctly write the vocabulary items on the board.

• Finally, invite volunteers to illustrate each vocabulary item on the board.

1 Read and complete the sentences.
Students complete the sentences with the correct words.

Answers

1. fossil, 2. saves, 3. landfills, 4. Conserve, 5. planting, 6. pollute, 7. energy, 8. emissions

2 Look and label the actions.
Using the first letter of each word as a clue, students write the vocabulary phrase that corresponds to each icon.

Answers

1. conserve water, 2. save electricity, 3. pollute the environment, 4. reduce carbon emissions, 5. send garbage to landfills, 6. plant trees, 7. use clean energy, 8. use fossil fuels

Wrap-up
Students review actions with a game similar to *Pictionary*.

• Model the activity by drawing one of the actions from the unit on the board, for example, *recycle*. You cannot speak or write any words; you can only draw pictures.

• The student who guesses comes to the board and draws another action.

• The student who guesses comes up to the board next.

• Continue until all actions have been reviewed or all students have had a chance to play.

➡ **Workbook p. 136, Activities 3 and 4 (Review)**

🐝 Teaching Tip

Setting the Right Pace in the Classroom
Here are some tips on how to pace the lesson:

• Create a sense of urgency. Keeping a stopwatch on your desk helps to make students feel that they need to use their time efficiently. Use the stopwatch for appropriate activities.

• Make the goals clear. One way to avoid a clunky lesson is to make sure students know exactly what they are learning and doing for the day.

• Transition smoothly. Try to set up the next activity within the same step that finishes the previous activity. While students are completing one activity, pass out any materials, set up equipment, make a note of what comes next on the board or have instructional materials ready for fast finishers.

✔ **Homework Check!**

Workbook p. 136, Activities 3 and 4 (Review)

Answers

3 Read the actions and write the impact they have on the environment.

1. You're reducing carbon emissions. 2. You're sending less garbage to landfills. 3. You're conserving water.

4 Think Fast! Write two more similar exchanges in your workbook.

Answers will vary.

Warm-up

Students review the first conditional with a round-robin.

- Write the sentence *If something bad can happen, it will.* on the board.

- Say *Imagine you are in a supermarket waiting to pay. The line is very long and doesn't seem to be moving at all. So you move to another line. What always happens?* Elicit *That line slows down and the one you were in first starts to move faster!*

- Students form groups of three. Have them write five sentences using the first conditional.

- Groups take turns reading the beginning of their sentences, for example, *If I don't take my umbrella…* and the other students try to guess the words to complete the sentence, for example, *it will rain.* Students have two tries to guess. If they do, their group gets a point.

- Continue until all groups have read their sentences and others have tried to guess. The group with the most points wins.

∃ Read and circle the correct option.

Students choose the correct verb forms to complete the first conditional sentences.

Answers

1. make, 2. can make, 3. will have, 4. start, 5. choose, 6. will make, 7. cares, 8. will improve

◁ Unscramble the questions.

Students unscramble the words to form first conditional sentences.

Answers

1. What will happen if we throw trash on the ground? 2. What will happen if we pollute the air? 3. What will happen if we pollute the oceans? 4. What will happen if we recycle? 5. What will happen if we use clean energy?

Extension

Students review the first conditional with a mingle activity.

- Write the phrase *What will you do if…* on the board.

- Have students take out a piece of paper and write the starter question at the top and number from 1 to 10.

- Students finish the question with ten original phrases, each followed by a line. If students need some ideas, refer them to the unit or assist them, for example, *you are late for class? you lose your phone? your best friend moves away?*

- When students are finished, have them stand up, bringing their papers and pencils with them. They walk around the room, asking each question and recording answers.

- When students have completed their papers, have them share what they discovered about their classmates.

? Big Question

Students are given the opportunity to revisit the Big Question and reflect on it.

- Ask students to turn to the unit opener on page 41 and think about the question "How can we save the planet?"

- Ask students to think about the discussions they've had on the environment, the readings they've read and the mini documentary they made.

- Students form small groups to discuss the following:

  » *Are you concerned about the present state of the environment? Why or why not?*

  » *If temperatures continue to rise year after year, how will our lives be different in the future?*

  » *Do you think most people worry about the environment? Explain your opinion.*

  » *What can we do to help the environment?*

Scorecard

Hand out (and/or project) a *Scorecard*. Have students fill in their *Scorecards* for this unit.

▶ **Study for the unit test.**

4 What's your passion?

Grammar
Intensifiers: extremely, so, really, pretty, a bit
Already and *Yet*: Did you go to the festival <u>yet</u>? They <u>already</u> registered for the competition. She didn't see the movie <u>yet</u>.

Vocabulary
Fan Activities: be a fan of, be good at, collect action figures, dress up as characters, get an autograph, put on face paint, put up posters, stand in line, wear a hat, wear team colors

Reading
Understanding questions in a dialogue

Speaking
Asking questions as an active listener

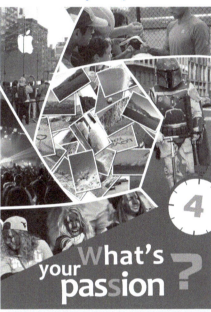

What's your passion?

In the first lesson, read the unit title aloud and have students look carefully at the unit cover. Encourage them to think about the message in the picture. At the end of the unit, students will discuss the big question: *What's your passion?*

 Teaching Tip

Personalizing Lessons

Students hear a lot of information in a school day. Communication opportunities in the language classroom offer a chance for students to talk about themselves and be a source of information. The topic of fan activities gives students the opportunity to talk about things they enjoy doing and why.

Vocabulary

Objective

Students will be able to use **fan activities** vocabulary to talk about things people do related to their hobbies and interests.

Lesson 1 Student's Book pp. 56 and 57

Warm-up

Students draw and write on the board things they enjoy doing.

- Write the Big Question in the center of the board: *What's your passion?*
- Invite as many students as possible to come to the board and write a few words, or draw a picture or symbol to represent an activity they enjoy doing or are a fan of.
- When they finish, other students come to the board and add to the phrases and pictures.
- Continue until all students have participated.

1 Look and underline the topic.

Students look at the photos to preview and identify the topic of the unit.

Answer

b

2 🎧¹⁶ Listen and number the expressions.

Students are exposed to **fan activities** vocabulary through a listening activity.

Answers

1. wear team colors, 2. put on face paint, 3. wear a hat, 4. be a fan of, 5. put up posters, 6. dress up as characters, 7. be good at, 8. collect action figures, 9. get an autograph, 10. stand in line

Audio Script

MR. STICKMAN: My passion is football! I can't wait for the fall when football season starts! It's fun to wear team colors on game day. They're green and yellow. I put on face paint, too. It's messy, but lots of fun. And I wear a silly hat for good luck.
ELSIE: I am a huge fan of zombies. I put up zombie posters all over my room. My friends and I dress up as movie characters. I'm really good at movie makeup, with fake blood and everything.
OWEN: I am a total Star Wars geek. I collect action figures—I have all of the main characters. I try to get autographs at conventions. I have Darth Vader's signature! I had to stand in line for three hours to get it!

3 🎧¹⁶ Read and complete the speech bubbles. Then listen again and check.

Students complete the vocabulary expressions with the words from the box.

Answers

Picture 1 colors, face, hat
Picture 2 fan, up, up, good
Picture 3 collect, get, in

Extension

Students guess fan activities based on objects from outside the classroom.

- Display objects related to fan activities: a hat with a sports logo, a poster, a mask, etc.
- Students form pairs and identify the related fan activities: *wear a hat, put up posters, dress up as characters*, etc.
- Then have the class vote for the activity they like most.

Wrap-up

Students play *Charades* to review fan activities vocabulary.

- Divide the class into three or four groups.
- One student in each group acts out a fan activity for the others to guess.
- Groups repeat with different volunteers acting out the vocabulary.

▐▐▶ Workbook p. 138, Activity 1

✔ Homework Check!

Workbook p. 138, Activity 1

Answers

1 Look and complete the phrases.

1. hat, 2. stand, 3. up, 4. at, 5. as, 6. get, 7. figures, 8. team, 9. fan

Warm-up

Students practice expressions with a treasure hunt.

• Write the two parts of each expression on separate pieces of paper, for example: *stand / in line.*

• Stick the pieces of paper around the room before class begins.

• When students come in, tell them they are going to have a treasure hunt. They should find both parts of each expression.

• After all students find all the expressions, have them read them aloud.

4 Read and match.

Students match the words in the two columns to complete the **fan activities**.

Answers

1. line, 2. at, 3. autograph, 4. as characters, 5. fan of, 6. colors, 7. action figures, 8. face paint, 9. hat, 10. posters

5 Read and complete the sentences.

Students complete sentences with vocabulary words and phrases.

Answers

1. team colors, 2. stand in line, 3. good at, 4. collect, 5. autographs, 6. wear, 7. dress up, 8. fan of

6 Describe the picture using the expressions from Activity 4.

Using the phrases they matched in Activity 4, students write their own descriptions of the photo of football fans.

7 Think Fast! Write the fan activities in alphabetical order. Which activities do you do?

Students do a three-minute timed challenge to practice **fan activities** vocabulary.

• Draw students' attention to the *Guess What!* box. Ask them if they have ever miss a character at the end of a book or movie? Fanfiction is a writing genre where people write stories about characters. They often imagine new adventures or invent alternate endings.

Extension

Students take a fan quiz.

• Make a fan quiz with information that applies to your city or country:

   » *Name something people stand in line for.*

   » *What are your school's / local sports team's team colors?*

   » *When do people dress up as characters?*

   » *Who do people ask for an autograph?*

   » *How many posters are in your room?*

• Form small teams and give them three minutes to answer all of the questions.

• The first team with answers for all of the questions wins. Elicit the answers.

Wrap-up

Students play a relay game to review **fan activities** vocabulary.

• Students form two teams and stand in two lines at the board.

• Give the first member of each team a marker.

• Say a vocabulary phrase. The first members write the first letter of the word and pass the marker to the next student. Each student in line adds a letter or makes a correction to a previous letter (only one change). The first team with the correctly spelled phrase wins a point.

• Continue with other vocabulary items.

▶ **Workbook p. 138, Activity 2**

🐝 Teaching Tip

Varying Activities to Reflect a Kinesthetic Learning Style

Students learn in different ways. Some are visual learners and respond well to information on the board, flashcards, pictures, worksheets and videos. Other students are auditory learners. These students learn best through songs, poems and riddles, verbal explanations and listening activities. Then there are kinesthetic learners. They respond well to movement. Just sitting and watching or listening won't keep them interested for long. Try to work in gestures when you teach new vocabulary. For example, when teaching the phrase *wear a silly hat*, mime the activity to teach and model, and have students do the same. When asking questions, toss a ball to "call on" students. Include craft and model-making activities when possible.

Grammar

Objective

Students will be able to use **intensifiers** and *already* and *yet* to talk about a special event.

Lesson 3   Student's Book p. 58

> ✔ Homework Check!
>
> Workbook p. 138, Activity 2
>
> **Answers**
> **2 Read and number.**
> *top to bottom* 7, 4, 5, 6, 1, 9, 8, 3, 2

Warm-up

Students discuss science fiction to generate interest and activate prior knowledge.

- Ask *What do you think of when you hear the words science fiction?* Accept any answers here.

➤ 60

- Write the following questions on the board:
  - » Do you like science fiction books and movies?
  - » What is the best science fiction book or movie in your opinion?
  - » What things do you think will never come true?
  - » If you wrote a sci-fi book, what would you write it about?
- Students form groups of three or four to discuss.

1 🎧¹⁷ **Read the flyer. Then listen and write C (Carrie) or A (Andrea).**

Students look at the photo and flyer, listen to the conversation and identify which speaker will dress up as each character.

Answers

1. Carrie, 2. Andrea

Audio Script

CARRIE: Wow! Look at this, Andrea!

ANDREA: Sci-Fi Festival. That's really cool! We should go!

CARRIE: Should we do the costume contest?

ANDREA: Of course! I'll dress up as... a robot, like from an old movie.

CARRIE: Mmm. That's a bit boring, don't you think?

ANDREA: You're right. How about a superhero? Wonder Woman?

CARRIE: That's a pretty good idea. What can I be?

ANDREA: Maybe River Song, from *Doctor Who*?

CARRIE: But the costume? I know—Katniss Everdeen, from the *Hunger Games*!

ANDREA: Carrie! That's an extremely cool idea! Maybe I can be Effie Trinket!

CARRIE: That's perfect! I can't wait! This is going to be so exciting!

---

2 🎧¹⁷ **Listen again and complete the phrases using intensifiers. What is the role of intensifiers?**

Students listen for and complete phrases with intensifiers from the audio.

Answers

1. cool, 2. boring, 3. good, 4. cool, 5. exciting; Intensifiers make adjectives stronger.

3 **Read and complete the dialogue.**

Using the ***Intensifiers*** box, students complete the dialogue with the intensifiers according to the cues.

Answers

1. pretty, 2. so / really, 3. extremely, 4. a bit

Wrap-up

Students personalize a discussion using intensifiers and play a game.

- Ask students to think of a sci-fi movie or other type of movie they've seen recently.
- Set a stopwatch for one minute. Students write as many adjectives as they can that describe the movie.
- Elicit the intensifiers from the lesson in order of intensity and write them on the board.
- Have students write the intensifiers on small individual pieces of paper about the size of index cards.
- Students form pairs, put their cards together in a single deck and place it face-down between them.
- The first student flips over one card. Using one of the adjectives and intensifier on the card, the student makes a statement about the movie. If the student is able to use the intensifier and one of the adjectives correctly, she keeps the card. If not, the other student gets a chance to use the intensifier and keep the card.
- Students continue until all intensifier cards are used. The student with the most cards wins.

➡ **Workbook p. 139, Activities 1 and 2**

✔ **Homework Check!**

Workbook p. 139, Activities 1 and 2

Answers

Answers

1 Number the intensifiers from least (0) to most intense (3).

1, 2, 3

2 Complete the dialogue using intensifiers.

1. so, 2. a bit, 3. pretty, 4. extremely

Warm-up

Students practice intensifiers by correcting mistakes.

• Write the following sentences on the board:

1. You look good really!
2. I hated that movie. It was a bit bad.
3. I did extremely well on the test. I got a C.

• Have students work in pairs to spot the mistakes and correct them.

Answers

1. You look really good! 2. It was extremely / so / really bad. 3. I did pretty well on the test.

4 🎧 ¹⁸ **Listen and mark (✓) the correct option.**

Students are exposed to usage of *already* and *yet* in a conversation and answer listening comprehension questions. Note: *already* and *yet* are often used in other tenses, but in American English, it's common to use them with the past simple.

Answers

1. an alien, 2. is, 3. didn't sign up, 4. already

_____

Audio Script

ELSIE: Hi, Jo! I love your alien costume!
Jo: Thanks, Elsie! Your costume is pretty cool, too! Are you a Jedi?
ELSIE: Yes. I'm Rey from Star Wars.
Jo: That's awesome. Did you sign up for the costume contest yet?
ELSIE: No, not yet. I'm going to do that right now.
Jo: I already signed up. It's really easy. I'll go with you!

_____

5 **Look at the map and write the sentences using *already* or *yet*.**

Students write sentences about activities Jo and Elsie have already done (marked with a checkmark on the map), or have not done yet (not marked on the map).

• Draw students' attention to the ***Already, Yet*** box and explain when we use each intensifier.

Answers

1. Jo and Elsie already played some games. 2. They didn't / did not have any snacks yet. 3. They didn't / did not watch a movie yet. 4. They already saw the fan art exhibition. 5. They already went to the costume contest.

6 **Think Fast!** **Imagine you are at the Sci-Fi Festival. Ask and answer five questions about the event.**

Students do a three-minute timed challenge: they form pairs and ask each other five questions about what activities they have already done or haven't done yet at the festival.

Wrap-up

Students practice *already* and *yet* with a card game.

• Have students take out a piece of paper and cut or tear it into nine pieces.

• Write these verbs on the board: *eat lunch, do your homework, clean your room, watch the movie, open your presents, make resolutions, go to the doctor, get his / her autograph, finish your project.*

• Students write one verb on each piece of paper until all the verbs are used.

• Students form pairs. They put their cards together, shuffle them and put them in a pile on the desk.

• Students choose a card and flip a coin. If the coin is heads, they make a sentence with the verb phrase and *already*. If it's tails, they make a sentence or question with the verb phrase and *yet*.

▐▐▐➡ **Workbook pp. 139 and 140, Activities 3–5**

61 ◀

Reading & Speaking

Objective
Students will be able to understand questions in a dialogue and ask questions as an active listener.

Lesson 5 Student's Book pp. 60 and 61

> ✔ **Homework Check!**
>
> Workbook p. 139 and 140, Activities 3–5
>
> **Answers**
>
> **3 Look and circle the correct option.**
> 1. No, they didn't. 2. Yes, they did.
>
> **4 Read and circle _T_ (True) or _F_ (False).**
> 1. F, 2. T, 3. F, 4. T
>
> **5 Unscramble and write.**
> 1. Did you watch a movie yet? 2. We already went to the art exhibition. 3. She already registered for the contest. 4. Did you already have some snacks?

➤ 62

Warm-up
Students brainstorm characteristics of a good listener to generate interest and activate prior knowledge.
- Write *Good Listener* on the board.
- Students form groups of three and brainstorm characteristics that describe a good listener.
- Come together as a class and have some students share their thoughts and ideas.

1 Read the descriptions. Which text describes a good listener?
Students read the descriptions of how people communicate and determine which text describes someone who listens well.
- Draw students' attention to the **Be Strategic!** box and read the information aloud.

Answer
1

2 Read the conversation and underline the questions.
Students identify the questions that are markers of active listening in a conversation.

Answers
What's your favorite activity, Renée? What are you passionate about? What do you do, I mean, as a cheerleader? What's that like? Is cheerleading a sport? How often do you work out? When is your next competition?

3 Complete and match.
Students complete the questions from Activity 2 and match each question with its answer.

Answers
1. do, We do cheers…, 2. like, It's a lot like gymnastics…, 3. Is, It is! 4. often, I go to the gym almost every day. 5. When, It's this Saturday.

Wrap-up
Students practice active listening with a classmate.
- Write several light topics on the board for students to talk about, for example, *pets, favorite food, favorite music,* etc.
- Students form pairs and choose a topic to discuss. When one student talks about the topic, the other should practice active listening by asking about details.
- Then they switch roles and have another conversation.

➠ **Workbook p. 141, Activities 1 and 2**

 Teaching Tip

Managing Fast Finishers
Some students complete activities more quickly than others, so it's a good idea to have a few extra activities on hand, otherwise these students may become bored and disruptive. One set of activities designed for fast finishers are the *Just for Fun* pages. Students can work on these individually and then check their answers in the back of the Student's Book. The *Just for Fun* activities for this unit are on page 68.

✔ **Homework Check!**

Workbook p. 141, Activities 1 and 2

Answers

1 Read and mark (✓) the topics in the article. Then circle the main idea of the article.

the history of the club, team colors, sponsors, the cost for fans, how to watch a game; *main idea:* the cost for fans

2 Read and match.

1. the location of one fan club, 2. a sponsor, 3. current team colors, 4. the name of a stadium, 5. $35, 6. $10

Warm-up

Students play a game to review *already* and *yet* with the past simple.

- Make two signs that say *already* and two signs that say *yet.* Place them in different parts of the classroom.

- Read a sentence or question, but clap in place of saying *already* or *yet,* for example, *I didn't have breakfast* [CLAP].

- Students should stand near the corresponding signs.

- Continue with other sentences and questions.

4 🎧¹⁹ **Read the dialogue and complete the questions. Then listen and check.**

Students listen to and complete a dialogue with examples of active listening.

Answers

what, How, When, where, Do

Audio Script

PATRICK: So what is your passion, Damian?
DAMIAN: My passion is train spotting. I am a total train geek. I love trains, and I learn everything about very specific engines. Then I go places to take pictures of them.
PATRICK: I don't know very much about train spotting. Aren't all trains the same? How are they different?
DAMIAN: Each engine is kind of unique. It has different colors and logos, according to the company it belongs to. And they have different numbers on them. They even have different horns.
PATRICK: When did you get interested in trains?
DAMIAN: When I was little.
PATRICK: And where do you go to see the trains?
DAMIAN: I go to many places, but my favorite place is by the river. It's a really great place for pictures.
PATRICK: Do you have a favorite picture?
DAMIAN: Yes. It's this one. A Union Pacific engine.
PATRICK: That's pretty cool. Hey, thanks for sharing about your hobby.
DAMIAN: You're welcome.

5 **Think Fast! Choose a dialogue to read aloud with a classmate. Can you do it without making any mistakes?**

Students do a five-minute timed challenge: they form pairs and read the dialogue from Activities 2 or 4 to each other.

6 **What are you passionate about? Ask and answer with a classmate.**

Students form pairs to practice active listening techniques as they have a conversation about something they are passionate about.

Stop and Think! Critical Thinking

What activities do you dislike? Is it ever good to do activities that are boring or unpleasant?

- Read the first question aloud: *What activities do you dislike?*

- Students form pairs and discuss.

- When students have finished, ask, *Is it ever good to do activities that are boring or unpleasant?*

- Have pairs suggest at least five activities.

- Come together as a class and have some students share their thoughts and ideas.

Wrap-up

Students conduct interviews with each other.
- Monitor, offering help as needed.

- Have students form pairs and take turns interviewing each other.

- Have each student tell the class about the person they interviewed, describing his / her passion.

➠ **(No homework today.)**

Preparing for the Next Lesson

Ask students to watch an introduction to village life in Pakistan: https://goo.gl/83nusO or invite them to look around on the web site: http://goo.gl/ANAVHt.

 *Culture*

Objectives

Students will be able to talk about the country of Pakistan and a popular sport there—street cricket.

 Lesson 7   Student's Book p. 62

Warm-up

Students are introduced to a topic with the game Two Truths and a Lie.

- Write the following facts on the board:

  » *Karachi, the largest city in Pakistan, is the capital.* (LIE—Islamabad is the capital, with just over one million people.)

  » *The official language of Pakistan is English.*

  » *The official currency of Pakistan is the rupee.*

- Students guess which one is the lie.

- Challenge students to guess the correct information.

> **64**

1 Look at the map. Do you know what country it is?

Students look at the map and guess what country it is.

Answer

Pakistan

2 Read and number.

Students read the facts about Pakistan and number the photos to match each one to the fact it illustrates.

Answers

left column 5, 6, 7, 3
right colum 8, 4, 2, 1

3 🎧²⁰ Listen and complete the table.

Students listen to the description of the games of cricket and street cricket in Pakistan and complete the table.

Answers

Cricket eleven
Street Cricket 70s, five, tennis, bat, street

Audio Script

Cricket has a long history in Pakistan. The British introduced the sport in the 18th century. Cricket teams compete on an international level. For those who aren't familiar with it, cricket is a game similar to baseball played on a cricket *pitch*, or field. There are eleven players on each team. The main equipment is a hard leather ball and a wooden bat, but players also wear protective pads, helmets and gloves. Schools and universities often have their own teams. In the 1970s, street cricket became popular in Pakistan. Players don't play on a pitch; they play in the street. There are only five players on each team. They don't use a lot of equipment— just a bat and a ball. The ball isn't leather; it's a tennis ball with electrical tape on it to make it stronger. Many famous Pakistani cricket players started out playing street cricket.

Wrap-up

Students discuss informal sports in their country.

- Point out that street cricket is popular because it doesn't use a lot of equipment. People can play it in the street.

- Ask *What sports in your country are popular because they don't use a lot of equipment?*

- Students form pairs and answer the question.

▐▐▐▶ **(No homework today.)**

Warm-up

Students make a KWL Chart to review and preview the topic.

- Draw a KWL Chart on the board, similar to following:

What I Know	What I Want to Know	What I Have Learned

- Ask students to think about what they know about Pakistan and what they want to know. Elicit some ideas. Students should not complete the chart yet. Instead, have them set it aside to use at the end of the lesson.
- Refer students to the texts on pages 62 and 63.

◀ **4   Read the article and write the headlines.**

Students read the text about Pakistan and match each headline with the appropriate paragraph.

Answers

Agriculture in Pakistan, An Annual Event, Sports, Other Attractions

5   Find and write the word.

Students scan the texts in Activities 2 and 4 about Pakistan to identify each item.

Answers

1. Pakistani, 2. Karachi, Islamabad, Lahore, 3. field hockey, 4. Malala Yousafzai, 5. manufacturing soccer balls, 6. mango, 7. spring, 8. horse

Stop and Think! Value

How are farmers important to a community?

- Ask *What do you eat every day?* Elicit some answers and write the foods and drinks on the board.
- Ask *Where does this food come from?* Accept any reasonable answers. Elicit the fact that yogurt, milk and cheese come from cows, cereal is a grain, meat is from farm animals, etc.
- Ask, *How are farmers important to a community?*
- Students form groups of three or four to discuss.
- Come together as a class and have some students share their ideas and thoughts.

Extension

Students quiz each other on a reading.

- Students form pairs and think of three questions about Pakistan.
- Two pairs form a group and take turns quizzing each other with questions. Challenge students not to look at the texts.
- Each correct answer earns the pair a point.
- When the first sets of pairs have finished, students rotate to another pair and quiz each other.
- The pair with the most points wins.

Wrap-up

Students complete their KWL Charts.

- Students take out their KWL Charts and complete the final column.
- Students form small groups of three or four and share what they have learned.
- Encourage students to discuss some of the following questions:
  - » What was the most interesting thing you learned?
  - » What was the most surprising thing you learned?
  - » Come together as a class and have some students share their thoughts and ideas.

▐▐▐➡ **(No homework today.)**

 *Project*

Objectives
Students will be able to make a fan activities brochure.

Lesson 9 Student's Book pp. 64 and 65

Warm-up
Students brainstorm words to generate interest and activate prior knowledge.
- Write the words *sports fan* on the board.
- Set a stopwatch for two minutes.
- Students form pairs and make as many words as they can from the letters on the board.
- When the stopwatch goes off, check that students have spelled all words correctly.
- Award one point for each correctly spelled word and two points for each word that is related to sports.

 66
- The pair with the most points wins.

1 Look at the Fan Activities brochure. Who is this brochure for?
Students skim the brochure and identify its audience.

Answers

sports fans, science fans, international food fans

2 Read the brochure and circle the correct option.
Students read the brochure and answer comprehension questions by choosing the words that complete each sentence correctly.

Answers

1. Boston, 2. baseball, 3. hockey, 4. observatory, 5. Ethiopian

3 Choose a city or region and complete the mind map. What kinds of fans are happy there? What activities can they do?
Students complete a mind map about a city or region, similar to the information in the brochure.

Wrap-up
Students present the information in their mind maps.
- Students form groups of three and share the information in their mind maps.
- Encourage students to ask each other questions and to give feedback.
- Monitor, offering help as needed.

 Teaching Tip

Teaching Students to Plan and Organize
Learning to organize information can help students far beyond the language classroom. Lists and mind maps are a good tool for this. Keep in mind that students might not be familiar with this, so working together with examples is a good start. Later on, students can make their own lists and mind maps for projects and writing tasks.

Warm-up

Students review their mind maps.

- Draw students' attention to their mind maps.
- Students form pairs and explain their mind maps to each other.

◀ **Make a Fan Activities brochure and present it to the class.**

Students make and present their brochures using the information in their mind maps.

The Digital Touch

To incorporate digital media in the project, suggest one or more of the following:

- Use your Microsoft Word to make a brochure: http://goo.gl/7G3SG8.
- Make your brochure online: https://goo.gl/KOBo2I.

Note that students should have the option to do the task on paper or digitally.

Extension

Students use the information in their brochures to role-play tour guides.

- Have students take out their travel brochures and identify the highlights of the place featured.
- If necessary, students do additional research to prepare a tour of the place.
- Students form groups of four or five.
- Each student "gives a tour" of the place featured in the travel brochure.

Wrap-up

Students use their brochures in a role play.

- Write the following conversation starter on the board: *Good morning. I'm interested in going to…*
- Elicit a city or place, for example, *Boston.*
- Then ask *Where do you think this conversation might take place?* Elicit *at a travel agency.*
- Ask students what the response might be. Elicit, for example, *OK. When would you like to go?*
- Continue eliciting a few statements until your students are ready to come up with a dialogue on their own.
- Students form pairs and role-play travel agent and customer, using their brochures.
- After students have finished their role play, have them switch roles.
- If time permits, have students form new pairs for more practice.

 67 ◀

▐▐▶ **Workbook p. 140, Activity 1 (Review)**

 **Review**

Objective

Students will be able to consolidate their understanding of the vocabulary and grammar learned in the unit.

Lesson 11   Student's Book pp. 66 and 67

> ✔ *Homework Check!*
>
> Workbook p. 140, Activity 1
>
> **Answers**
>
> **1 Read and correct the sentences.**
>
> 1. ~~of~~ My friends and I dress up <u>as</u> characters. 2. ~~on~~ My sister put <u>up</u> posters in her room. 3. ~~up~~ For big games, we put <u>on</u> face paint. 4. ~~in~~ Ryan is really good <u>at</u> dancing. 5. ~~at~~ I stood <u>in</u> line for three hours.

Warm-up

Students review **fan activities** vocabulary with a game similar to *Pictionary*.

- Model the activity by drawing one of the vocabulary items on the board, for example, *wear a silly hat*. You cannot speak or write any words; you can only draw pictures.
- The student who guesses comes to the board and draws another action.
- The student who guesses comes up to the board next.
- Continue until all actions have been reviewed or all students have had a chance to play.

1 **Complete the questions. Then read and match.**

Students complete the vocabulary phrases in the questions and match the questions and answers.

Answers

1. action, Yes! I collect… 2. good, I'm good at drawing… 3. get, When I was little… 4. stand, Maybe for half an hour… 5. fan, I'm a fan of… 6. dress, Only on Halloween!…

2 **Look and write a fan activity.**

Students write the activity vocabulary phrase that each photo illustrates.

Answers

1. put on face paint, 2. put up posters, 3. wear a hat, 4. stand in line

3 **Read and underline the intensifiers. Write them on the lines.**

Students identify the intensifiers in the text.

Answers

1. extremely, 2. really, 3. a bit, 4. so, 5. pretty

4 **Look and write !, !!, !!! or !!!! next to the intensifiers.**

Students determine how strong each intensifier in Activity 3 is.

Answers

1. !!!!, 2. !!!, 3. !, 4. !!!, 5. !!

Wrap-up

Students do a mingle to practice asking and answering questions.

- Have students write *Find Someone Who…* on the top of a piece of paper.
- Draw students' attention to the questions in Activity 1.
- Using the questions, students write phrases that follow *find someone who…* Students should produce phrases similar to the following:
  - » *… collects action figures.*
  - » *… is good at cheerleading / train spotting.*
  - » *… got an autograph from someone.*
  - » *… stood in line for something for over an hour.*
  - » *… is a fan of international food / music / sports / history / art and literature.*
  - » *… dressed up as a character.*
- When students have finished writing their phrases, have them stand up, mingle and ask and answer questions.
- Make note of any mistakes in pronunciation, grammar or vocabulary for an anonymous feedback session after the activity.

▐▐▐▶ **Workbook p. 140, Activity 2 (Review)**

✔ Homework Check!

Workbook p. 140, Activity 2

Answers

2 Read and complete the sentences.

1. yet, 2. yet, 3. already, 4. yet

Warm-up

Students play a game to practice intensifiers:

- Have students stand up.

- Say a sentence with an intensifier, for example, *Boston is really exciting*.

- Indicate that the student near you should repeat the sentence, changing the intensifier, for example, *Boston is extremely exciting*.

- Continue using all of the intensifiers from this unit. Change sentences as needed.

5 Read and describe using intensifiers. Choose and circle the adjective.

Students practice using intensifiers and adjectives together to describe their own opinions.

Answers

Answers will vary.

6 Write sentences using the cues and *already* or *yet*.

Students review the usage of *already* and *yet* by writing sentences using the cues.

Answers

1. We already saw the fan art exhibition. 2. Sam didn't / did not get the concert tickets yet. 3. Did Allison watch the new movie yet? 4. Did you complete your costume yet? 5. They didn't / did not read the book yet.

Extension

Students review with a game called *Kaboom!*

- For this game, you will need balloons, one for each student in your class.

- Write review questions or items on slips of paper and place each in a balloon. Here are some review items:

  » *I like to _____ team colors to games.*

  » *Which intensifier is stronger than so?*

  » *Do you _____ Legos?*

  » *Already or yet? I _____ ate breakfast.*

- Give each student a balloon and have him / her blow it up and attach it to his / her shoe.

- Students then mingle and try to pop each other's balloons.

- The student who pops the balloon takes out the review question and asks the question to the student whose balloon was popped.

- If the student can answer the question or complete the item, she can continue trying to pop other students' balloons. If not, she must sit down and is out of the game.

- Continue until there is only one student left with a balloon. That student is the winner.

 **Big Question**

Students are given the opportunity to revisit the Big Question and reflect on it.

- Ask students to turn to the unit opener on page 55 and think about the question "What's your passion?"

- Ask students to think about the discussions they've had on people's interests and passions, the readings they've read and the brochure they made.

- Students form small groups to discuss the following:

  » What is your passion?

  » How much time do you spend doing that activity? Is it enough?

  » Do you think it's important to have a passion? Why or why not?

- Monitor, offering help as needed, particularly with vocabulary.

 Scorecard

Hand out (and/or project) a *Scorecard*. Have students fill in their *Scorecards* for this unit.

⫸ **Study for the unit test.**

5 How much do you remember?

Grammar

Past Continuous: The children <u>were playing</u> all day. My computer <u>wasn't working</u> yesterday.

Past Continuous with Past Simple and *When*: The family was swimming <u>when</u> strong currents <u>pulled</u> them away from the beach.

***While*:** I <u>was reading</u> a book <u>while</u> my dad <u>was watching</u> TV.

Vocabulary

Personal Experiences: buy a lot of souvenirs, fall in love, forget, get in trouble, get lost, have a lot of fun, make a mistake, take care of

Keepsakes: baby tooth, drawing, necklace, seashell, toy car

Reading

Making connections between images and text

Writing

Completing an outline

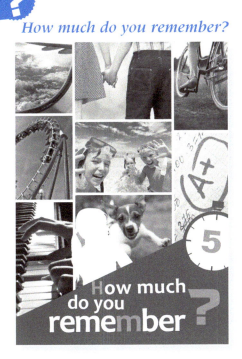

In the first lesson, read the unit title aloud and have students look carefully at the unit cover. Encourage them to think about the message in the picture. At the end of the unit, students will discuss the big question: *How much do you remember?*

🗯 Teaching Tip

Learning Outside the Classroom

Learning a language is like riding a bike or learning a musical instrument: the more you do it, the better you can get. In the classroom, we try to give students as much opportunity to practice and use English as possible, but they are more likely to succeed if they use English outside the classroom. Encourage students to seek out TV programs, websites and books in English. Even product labels in English can be a good way for students to learn. More advanced students can try putting their phone or email settings in English. These strategies will make English a regular part of students' everyday lives and help them to use it effectively in the future.

 **Vocabulary**

Objective

Students will be able to use **Personal Experiences** and **Keepsakes** vocabulary to talk about memories.

Lesson 1   Student's Book pp. 70 and 71

Warm-up

Students ask and answer about personal experiences and keepsakes to build interest in the unit topic.

- Display photos and/or keepsakes: souvenirs from trips, postcards, etc. Choose interesting items that you feel comfortable showing to the class.

- Invite students to look at the items (without picking them up) and ask questions about them.

- Write *Memories* on the board. Tell students to think about one of their favorite past experiences (memories). Ask *Where were you? Who was there? Why was it special?*

 72

- After everyone has had time to think, elicit answers from volunteers.

1 Look and number the pictures.

Students match photos of situations with statements describing each experience.

Answers

top to bottom 4, 5, 1, 7, 6, 8, 2, 3

2 Read and circle the correct option.

Students choose the verb phrase that best completes each sentence.

Answers

1. took care of, 2. made a mistake, 3. got in trouble, 4. bought, 5. fell in love with

Wrap-up

Students review collocations with a game of *Go Fish.*

- Have students take out two pieces of paper and cut or tear each into eight pieces so there are sixteen pieces altogether.

- Students write the two parts of each collocation on separate cards: *take / care of, make / a mistake, have / a lot of fun, forget / something, get in / trouble, get / lost, buy / something, fall / in love with.* Note that they should write lightly in pencil, so that the words are not visible through the paper.

- Students form small groups. They place their cards in a pile and deal five cards to each player. The remaining cards go into a lake at the center of the group.

- The first student asks another student for a word or phrase corresponding to one of the cards in his or her hand, for example, *care of.* If the student has the card, he gives it to him or her to complete the phrase: *take care of.* If the student does not have the

card, he or she says *Go fish!* The first student then draws a card from the lake.

- If the player forms a phrase, the student keeps the pair and plays again. If not, the next student plays.

- Continue playing until all cards have been matched correctly.

- The student with the most phrases wins.

▐▐▶ **Workbook p. 142, Activity 1**

✔ Homework Check!

Workbook p. 142, Activity 1

Answers

1 Look, read and number.

top row 2, 3; *bottom row* 5, 1, 4

Warm-up

Students discuss the idea of keepsakes to generate interest and activate prior knowledge.

- Write *keepsake* on the board. Underline *keep* and ask students if they know what *keepsake* means.

- Elicit or provide that *a keepsake is an item kept to help you remember a person or an experience.*

- Write the following questions on the board:

  » Do you have any keepsakes? What are they?

- Students form pairs and discuss.

- Come together as a class and have some students share their thoughts and ideas.

3 🎧²¹ **Listen and match the people with the keepsakes.**

Students determine which person discusses each keepsake.

Answers

1. drawing, 2. necklace, 3. seashell, 4. toy car, 5. baby tooth

___

Audio Script

One

TEEN BOY: My keepsake is a picture that I drew when I was seven years old. It shows a dinosaur with big teeth.

Two

WOMAN: My keepsake is this old necklace. It was my grandmother's. When I was little, I found it in her room and asked to put it on, so she gave it to me. It's very special.

Three

BOY: I found this seashell on the beach, on a trip with my family. I took it to school once to show my class. Now I keep it in a box under my bed.

Four

OLD MAN: My keepsake is a toy from my childhood. It's a car. You turned this key to make it go, you see. It's red and not in perfect condition anymore. I think it was my father's when he was a child.

Five

YOUNG GIRL: My keepsake is a baby tooth. I was six years old when I had my first loose tooth. I was very nervous about pulling it. Then one day, it just fell out!

4 **Read the description. Then write the name of the keepsake.**

Students match the descriptions with the photos of keepsakes in Activity 3.

- Draw students' attention to the *Guess What!* box. Tell them that photos and keepsakes—objects from important events—are common ways to remember the past. But music, smells and flavors can also help you remember information and experiences.

Answers

1. necklace, 2. toy car, 3. seashell, 4. baby tooth, 5. drawing

5 **Think Fast!** **Classify the keepsakes.**

Students do a one-minute timed challenge: they put each keepsake from the previous activities into a category in the table.

Answers

drawing, necklace, toy car, baby tooth, seashell

Wrap-up

Students make and put together a puzzle with a keepsake item.

- Students form pairs and draw a keepsake item on a sheet of paper. For an added challenge, they can draw two items, one on each side.

- Students cut their picture into medium-sized pieces (about 15) and exchange puzzles with another pair.

- Have students put the puzzle together and identify the item. If it is two-sided, have them mix up the puzzle and put together the other picture.

- As they work, encourage them to talk about keepsake items that they have.

▐▐▶ **Workbook p. 142, Activities 2 and 3**

🗨 **Teaching Tip**

Balancing Competition and Collaboration

Both competitive and cooperative activities have a place in the classroom. Competition, where teams compete and one team or one student wins, can engage and motivate students. However, if used improperly, competition can shift focus from the learning process to winning, and can increase anxiety, especially in shy students. Collaboration, on the other hand, does not involve points or winning. Students work together to complete a task. In these activities, it may be necessary to monitor students and help them stay focused. Some students participate better in collaborative activities.

Grammar

Objective

Students will be able to use the **present continuous** to talk about ongoing past activities. They will also be able to use the **present continuous** with *while* to talk about simultaneous activities in the past and the **past simple** with *when* for interrupted activities in the past.

Lesson 3   Student's Book p. 72

> ✔ Homework Check!
>
> Workbook p. 142, Activities 2 and 3
>
> **Answers**
> **2 Find and circle the names of five keepsakes.**
> baby tooth, drawing, seashell, toy car
> **3 Complete the sentences using the words from Activity 2.**
> 1. baby teeth, 2. drawing, 3. seashell, 4. toy car

74 | Warm-up

Students think about the context of the past continuous by recalling the previous day's activities.

- Draw a simple timetable on the board with four or five different times covering morning, afternoon and evening.

- Tell students to try to remember their day yesterday in as much detail as possible. Ask *What were you doing at (seven) o'clock?* Do not elicit answers. Give students a moment to think. Encourage them to remember the situation in as much detail as they can.

- Repeat with other questions.

- Elicit answers from a few volunteers. Do not correct grammar at this point.

1 Look and number the scenes.

Students number the drawings to put the scenes in narrative order.

Answers

1. It's a beautiful day! 2. We're going for a swim. 3. Look! we're really far from the beach. 4. Help! Help! 5. Stay calm and we'll get you out.

2 🎧²² Listen and underline the cause of the problem.

Students listen to the narrative and identify the cause of the swimmers' problem.

Answer

c

Audio Script

Good morning. This is the six o'clock news. Three members of a family were swimming near Lookout Beach yesterday morning when they got into trouble. Strong currents pulled the swimmers away from the beach and it wasn't possible for them to swim back. Other family members were relaxing at the beach when they realized there was a problem and raised the alarm. Local lifeguards were teaching a first-aid course when they heard the dad shouting for help. They managed to get to the swimmers quickly and rescue them. Lifeguard Matt Fry said, "When we located the family, the two children were crying and the uncle was trying to calm them down. All three of them were pretty exhausted." The uncle, Ken Wise, said, "I wasn't paying attention. We were swimming and having fun and we didn't realize the current was so strong. When my niece saw we were so far from the beach, it was very hard to swim back. We were very lucky that the lifeguards were nearby."

3 🎧²² Listen again and circle *T* (True) or *F* (False).

Students listen again for detail and identify whether statements about the story are true or false.

Answers

1. T, 2. F (They were having fun.), 3. F (The dad raised the alarm.), 4. T, 5. F (The two children were crying.)

4 Think Fast! Find and underline the verbs in the past continuous in Activity 3.

Students do a one-minute timed activity: they identify the past continuous verbs in Activity 3 and underline them.

- Draw students' attention to the **Past Continuous** box and explain the use.

Answers

1. was relaxing, 2. weren't having fun, 4. were teaching, 5. was crying

Wrap-up

Students cooperate to complete a story.

- Write the following story starter on the board: *Last summer I went camping. I was putting up my tent when…*

- Students form small groups and complete the story, with one member acting as secretary.

- Elicit students' stories.

▐▶ **Workbook p. 143, Activities 1 and 2**

✔ Homework Check!

Workbook p. 143, Activities 1 and 2

Answers

1 Look and answer the questions.

1. Yes, they were. 2. No, she wasn't. 3. No, they weren't. 4. Yes, he was.

2 Look again and write sentences using *while*.

1. Alan was sleeping while Bill was reading. 2. Miss Smith was writing while Claire, Emma and Pam were paying attention. 3. Bill was reading while Gina and Hal were giving a presentation.

Warm-up

Students practice past continuous with a collaborative silly story-writing activity.

- Invite students to write verbs and verb phrases on the board, for example, *blow out candles.*

- Students form small groups. Tell them to choose five verbs or verb phrases from the board and use them to write a silly story. They must use three of the verbs in the present continuous tense. One member acts as the group secretary. Monitor and help as needed.

- Elicit students' stories. Have them set aside their stories to use in the *Wrap-up* activity.

5 Match the parts of the sentences.

Students match the beginnings and endings of sentences from the story about the swimmers.

- Draw students' attention to the **Past Continuous and Past Simple**: **When** box and explain the difference between the tenses.

Answers

1. when they got into trouble. 2. when they realized there was a problem and raised the alarm. 3. when they heard the dad shouting for help. 4. the children were crying.

6 Read the excerpts and write the headings.

Students read parts of news articles and identify the natural disaster each is about.

- Draw students' attention to the **Guess What!** box. Tell them that when we talk about two simultaneous actions in the past, we use while: I was reading a book while my dad was watching TV.

Answers

top to bottom A tornado, An earthquake, A flood

7 Read the underlined sentences in Activity 6. Then write *S* (Simultaneous) or *I* (Interrupted).

Students identify whether the two actions described in each sentence are happening simultaneously or whether one action interrupts another.

Answers

1. S, 2. S, 3. I, 4. S, 5. I, 6. S, 7. I, 8. I

Extension

Students play a game to review *when* and *while.*

- Students form groups of three. When one student says *Go!*, the other two students each say a verb, for example, *exercising* and *eating cake.*

- The student must make a *when* or *while* sentence using the verbs, such as *While he was exercising, he was eating cake.* The student can use either *when* or *while*, depending on the verbs.

- Students switch roles and play again. They should repeat the game several times.

Wrap-up

Students revise their stories to add details and incorporate *when* and *while.*

- Students form the groups that they were in for the *Warm-up* activity and take out their stories.

- Have students reread their stories and add details using the present continuous and *when* or *while.* Monitor and help as needed.

- Elicit students' stories.

▶ **Workbook p. 144, Activity 3**

 **Reading & Listening**

Objective

Students will be able to make connections between images and text and make an outline.

Lesson 5   Student's Book pp. 74 and 75

✔ **Homework Check!**

Workbook p. 144, Activity 3

Answers

3 Write sentences using *when*.

1. She was walking her dog when she saw an accident. 2. He was riding his bike when his telephone rang. 3. They were studying for a math exam when someone knocked at the door.

Warm-up

Students do a memory exercise to build interest in the topic.

- Write a sequence of numbers on the board: *32-15-27-85.*
- Students form groups and determine a strategy for remembering the sequence of numbers. They are not allowed to write them down.
- Elicit students' strategies. Then give them two minutes to memorize the sequence.
- Erase the numbers on the board. Invite volunteers to stand and recite the sequence of numbers.
- Then ask questions that involve numbers to distract students from the sequence: *When is your birthday? What time is it? How old are you?*

1 Look and mark (✓) the topic of the article.

Students read the title of the article and look at the photo to determine the topic.

Answer

the parts of the brain and memory

2 Read the article and label.

Students read the article and use the information to determine the correct label for each picture.

- Draw students' attention to the **Be Strategic!** box and read the information aloud.

Answers

network, neuron, the cerebral cortex, the hippocampus

3 Read again and complete the sentences.

Students read for detail and complete the sentences with information from the article.

Answers

1. cells, 2. electricity, 3. connections, 4. neurons, 5. hippocampus, 6. cerebral, 7. replays

Extension

Students demonstrate understanding of the reading with a flow chart.

- Draw a flow chart on the board similar to the following:

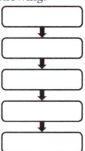

- Explain that this is a flow chart that can be used to summarize a process.
- Students form pairs and underline the key points in the reading to add to the flow chart.
- When students have finished, have them meet with another pair and share their flow charts.

Wrap-up

Encourage students to discuss some of the following questions:

» What was the most surprising thing you learned?

» In the article, it says that you can remember words to songs more easily because they are connected to music. Have you experienced this? Give some examples.

- Monitor, offering help as needed.
- Come together as a class and have some students share their thoughts and ideas.

➠ **Workbook p. 145, Activities 1 and 2**

Lesson 6
Student's Book p. 75

✔ **Homework Check!**

Workbook p. 145, Activities 1 and 2

Answers

1 Read and underline two hormones that affect your body clock.

melatonin, cortisol

2 Read again and mark the times for each activity on the timeline.

4, 3, 1, 2

Warm-up

Students identify the main idea and details in the text to review.

- Draw students' attention to the reading on page 74.
- Elicit the topic of the text: *the parts of the brain and memory.*
- Write these sentences on the board.
  1. The brain is an organ that works like a very powerful computer.
  2. When you learn something, new connections form between neurons.
  3. This is the "skin" of the brain.
  4. For example, you can easily remember the lyrics to your favorite song…
- Students form pairs and determine whether the sentences give main ideas or details. Elicit the answers: *1. M, 2. M, 3. D, 4. D*

4 🎧²³ Listen and circle the correct option.

Students listen and circle the word that completes each sentence in the notes.

Answers

1. technology, 2. healthy, 3. first, 4. things, 5. Give

Audio Script

Did you forget your homework recently? Do you have trouble remembering names, dates or facts? Nowadays, it's easy to let technology remember for you. Your phone is an address book, a calendar and even an encyclopedia. And you can look up most information online, so why remember? Remembering keeps your brain active and healthy. Like a muscle, your brain is stronger when you use it. So how can you remember better? The first strategy is to take care of yourself: get enough sleep, eat a healthy diet and manage stress through exercise and meditation. OK, so you take care of yourself. Now what? Write things down. Not on a phone or a computer. Write using a pen or pencil. Science shows that this helps you to remember, even if you don't look at your notes. Or give your brain a job: teach the information to another person. You repeat the information, building more neuron connections. You can also identify information that you need to learn or review.

5 🎧²³ Read and complete the notes in Activity 4. Then listen again and check.

Students write the phrases from the box under the sentences they go with and listen to the audio again to check their notes.

Answers

1. your phone, information online, 2. like a muscle, 3. enough sleep, healthy diet, manage stress, 4. pen or pencil, 5. teach someone

6 Think Fast! Choose one item and try to memorize the information. Can you remember it when time is up?

Students do a three-minute timed challenge: they pick one of the notes from Activities 4 and 5 and try to memorize it. After three minutes, they try to recall the information.

- Draw students' attention to the *Guess What!* box. Tell them that mnemonic devices are strategies to help you remember specific information. For example, making a chant or song can help you to remember lists or names.

Wrap-up

Students personalize the lesson with a discussion.

- Draw students' attention to the items in Activity 4. Say *Reread the tips for helping your memory be better.*
- Write the following questions on the board:
  » Do you use any of these tips? Which ones?
  » Can you suggest other tips for remembering things?
- Students form small groups and discuss the questions.
- Come together as a class and have some students share their thoughts and ideas.

➡ **Workbook p. 145, Activity 3**

Preparing for the Next Lesson

Ask students to watch an Aboriginal artist at work https://goo.gl/THCrcB or listen to an explanation of an Aboriginal musical instrument at https://goo.gl/Zu3ndb.

 **Culture**

Objectives

Students will be able to talk about Aboriginal Australians and the Great Barrier Reef.

Lesson 7 Student's Book p. 76

✔ **Homework Check!**

Workbook pp. 145, Activity 3

Answers

3 Think Fast! In your notebook, draw a timeline about your day.
Answers will vary.

Warm-up

Students complete a simple map of Australia.

- Draw an outline of Australia on the board.

- Mark the locations of these important Australian cities with dots: *Melbourne, Sydney, Brisbane, Perth, Adelaide.* Mark the location of Canberra with a star. Do not write the names on the map.

- Write the names of the cities next to the map. Encourage students to guess the location of each city.

- Write the first letter for each city on the map and invite volunteers to complete the names. Elicit the name of the capital city: *Canberra*.

1 Read and complete the sentences.

Students learn facts about Aboriginal Australians by completing sentences with the options provided.

Answers

1. forty-five thousand, 2. 3%, 3. Ayers Rock, 4. didgeridoo, 5. kangaroo

2 Read the article. Then write the underlined words under the correct images.

Students read the article and write captions for the photos, using the words they find underlined in the text.

Answers

Uluru, rock paintings, body painting, dot painting

Wrap-up

Students prepare a quiz based on the text.

- Write the following question on the board: *What do Aboriginal Australians call the period that is the beginning of creation? (Dreamtime).*

- Students form pairs. They come up with eight questions about the text to quiz their classmates. Be sure that both students in each pair write down their questions.

- Tell students to remember to make an answer key.

- Have students form new pairs and quiz each other on the text.

▶ **(No homework today.)**

 **Teaching Tip**

Promoting Multiculturalism in the Classroom

Creating a safe, accepting and successful learning environment for all students is only one result of promoting multiculturalism in your classroom. When you expose students to various cultures, you are helping them become more aware of global issues. You also stimulate critical thinking and reduce prejudice and discrimination. Here are two ways you can integrate multicultural education into your classroom:

- Create multicultural projects that require students to choose a background different from their own. This can include research projects, book reports and role plays.

- Supplement your lessons with current events and news stories so you can draw parallels between cultures, displaying universal experiences.

Warm-up

Students make a KWL Chart to review what the know about Australia.

• Draw a KWL Chart on the board, similar to following:

What I Know	What I Want to Know	What I Have Learned

• Ask students to think about what they know about Australia and what they want to know. Elicit some ideas.

• Have students complete the chart. Then they should set it aside to use at the end of the lesson.

3 Look at the pictures. Do you know what place it is?
Students look at the photos and try to guess the place.

4 🎧²⁴ Listen and unscramble the name of the place.
Students listen and unscramble the three words that make up the name of the place.

Answers
Great Barrier Reef

Audio Script
INTERVIEWER: Hello and welcome to the program The Wonders of Nature. Today's guest comes all the way from Australia and he will talk to us about the Great Barrier Reef. Welcome, Steve Star.
STEVE STAR: Hello, thank you for having me.
INTERVIEWER: Tell us, where is the Great Barrier Reef?
STEVE STAR: It is located off the Queensland coast of Australia.
INTERVIEWER: How big is it?
STEVE STAR: It is 2,000 kilometers long and 180 meters high. It consists of 3,000 individual reefs and 900 islands. It is as big as 70 million football fields!
INTERVIEWER: Oh, no! I can't imagine anything like it! What is is made of?
STEVE STAR: It is made of coral, and coral is formed of thousands of little creatures called polyps.
INTERVIEWER: How many types of fish live there?
STEVE STAR: 1,500 types. There are also 26 types of whales and dolphins, 100 types of starfish and many more.
INTERVIEWER: Are there any threats to the Great Barrier Reef?
STEVE STAR: The GBR faces several threats, some caused by humans and some by nature itself. For example, ships running around the reef destroy parts of it. Tourists kill the reef by visiting it, littering, etc. The natural threat is the Crown-of-thorns starfish that eats the polyps.
INTERVIEWER: Is the GBR a Natural Wonder of the World?

STEVE STAR: Yes, it is.
INTERVIEWER: Wow! And finally, is it true that you can see it from outer space?
STEVE STAR: Yes! Astronauts can see it from the Moon. They say you can see a white fine line in the blue ocean…

---

5 🎧²⁴ Listen again and number the questions in order.
Students number the questions according to the audio.

Answers
first column 5, 6, 1, 7
second column 2, 4, 3

6 Match the questions with the answers.
Students write the numbers of the questions in Activity 5 next to the corresponding answers.

Answers
1. 7/6, 2. 1, 3. 4, 4. 2, 5. 3, 6. 6/7, 7. 5

Stop and Think! Value
Are there natural wonders under threat in your country?

• Ask *What are the threats the GBR faces?*

• Then ask *What are some natural wonders in your country? Are they under threat?*

• Students form pairs and brainstorm answers. Elicit students' ideas.

Wrap-up

Students review facts about Australia.

• Students take out their KWL Charts and complete the final column.

• Students form small groups of three or four and share what they have learned.

• Encourage students to investigate the things they would still like to know about Australia.

▶ **(No homework today.)**

Project

Objectives

Students will be able to make a personalized timeline.

Lesson 9   Student's Book p. 78

Warm-up

Students talk about their life events to build interest in the project theme.

- Write *Life Events* on the board and elicit examples, such as *being born, starting school, traveling* or *moving to a different house.*

- Students form pairs and talk about their life events.

1 Look at the timeline on page 79 and choose the correct option.

Students answer the questions using information from the timeline on page 79.

Answers

1. a, 2. a, 3. c, 4. b, 5. a

2 Classify the events from Aaron's timeline. Write *PE* or *WE*.

Students identify whether each event from the timeline is a personal experience or a world event.

Answers

top to bottom WE, PE, PE, WE, WE, PE, WE, PE, PE, WE, PE, PE, WE, WE

3 List seven important personal events for you and your family. Write the dates.

Students think of and write seven events and the date each happened for their personal timelines.

Extension

Students identify important world events that happened in their lifetime.

- Draw students' attention to the timeline on page 79.

- Say *Look at your list of events and the dates in Activity 3. Find some important world events that happened during that period.*

- Students can do this at home, in the library or if you have computers in the classroom, allow them to do research in class. As an alternative, print off general information for students to use as they research.

- When students have completed their research, have them share and compare the important world events in pairs or small groups.

Wrap-up

Students quiz each other about the information in Aaron's timeline.

- Students form pairs. They take turns asking and answering questions about the timeline on page 79.

Warm-up

Students use a timeline to tell Aaron's story.

- Elicit sequencing words and write them on the board: *first, then, after that, next, finally.* Leave these on the board for later in the lesson.

- Draw students' attention to Aaron's timeline on page 79.

- Students form pairs. Using the sequence words and timeline, they take turns telling Aaron's story.

◁ **4 Make a personalized timeline. Use Aaron's timeline as a model.**

Using the timeline on page 79 as a model, students add to the events and dates they thought of in Activity 3 and use their own events to create a personalized timeline.

The Digital Touch

To incorporate digital media in the project, suggest one or more of the following:

- Create a digital timeline online with Timeline at http://goo.gl/HyDTHb. Timeline is also available as a free Apple or Android app.

Note that students should have the option to do a task on paper or digitally.

Extension

Students make a timeline to represent their weekend activities. Then they compare with another classmate.

- Tell students to draw a timeline to show their activities from the previous weekend. Encourage them to include ongoing activities, for example, *watching TV.*

- Students form pairs and use the past continuous with *when* and *while* to compare their activities, for example, *She was watching TV while I was reading a book.*

- Have volunteers read their sentences to the class.

Wrap-up

Students use a timeline to tell their story with sequence words.

- Draw students' attention to the sequencing words on the board.

- Students form pairs. Using the sequence words and their own timeline, they take turns telling each other their own stories.

- Have a few students share their stories with the class.

➠ **Workbook p. 144, Activity 1 (Review)**

Review

Objective
Students will be able to consolidate their understanding of the vocabulary and grammar learned in the unit.

Lesson 11 Student's Book p. 80

> ✔ **Homework Check!**
>
> Workbook p. 144, Activity 1
>
> **Answers**
>
> **1 Complete the table.**
>
> *Present Simple* prepare breakfast, drinks, buys souvenirs
>
> *Past Simple* got in trouble, drank, worked, had a lot of fun
>
> *Past Continuous* were getting in trouble, was preparing breakfast, was working, was buying souvenirs, were having a lot of fun

> **82** **Warm-up**

Students review vocabulary with a board relay race.

- Students form teams of five or six. Divide the board by drawing lines down the board to form as many columns as there are teams.

- Give each team a marker.

- Using the glossaries and suggested definitions below, say a definition for one of the vocabulary words.

- A member from each team writes a word on the board. Once a team member is finished writing the word, stop saying the definition.

- The students at the board each give the marker to another team member as in a relay race.

- Say another definition and follow the same procedure.

- When you have reviewed all the definitions, look at the students' answers.

- The team with the most complete and correctly spelled words wins.

1 Unscramble names of keepsakes. Then read and number the questions.

Students unscramble the keepsakes vocabulary words and match each to one of the questions below.

Answers

1. necklace, 2. baby tooth, 3. toy car, 4. drawing, 5. seashell; *top to bottom* 1, 5, 2, 4, 3

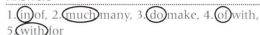

2 Circle and correct the mistakes.

Students review verb phrases by correcting the sentences.

Answers

1. in/of, 2. much/many, 3. do/make, 4. of/with, 5. with/for

3 Write sentences using the past simple.

Students complete the sentences in past simple using the cues.

Answers

1. forgot her name at the party. 2. bought a T-shirt at the stadium. 3. cell phone got lost during P.E. class. 4. had fun with our friends yesterday. 5. got in trouble for drawing on the wall. 6. made several mistakes in my German homework. 7. fell in love with my new computer.

Wrap-up
Students review past simple with a game of *Bingo*.

- Draw a grid on the board with nine squares.

- Have students take out a piece of paper and draw a similar grid.

- Tell students to write one past tense verb from the unit in each square.

- Say a past tense verb in its base form, for example, *forget*. If a student has *forgot* in a square, she marks it with an *X*.

- When a student has three *X*s, diagonally, horizontally or vertically, he or she shouts *Bingo!*

- The student must read the verbs back and use each in a sentence to win.

- Play several times.

▶ **(No homework today.)**

Warm-up

Students practice past simple and past continuous with a game called *Accusations*.

- Write a list of actions that are a little strange on the board, for example:
  - » *paint your windows blue*
  - » *give your cat a bath*
  - » *hit your phone with a hammer*
  - » *dig a big hole in the ground*

- Divide the class into two groups, Students A and Students B.

- Using the actions on the board, Student A asks Student B questions, for example, *When I saw you yesterday, you were painting your windows with blue paint. Why were you doing that?*

- Student B must invent a silly reason why she was going that, for example, *I was painting my house in team colors.*

- Student B then questions Student A, who answers.

- Come together as a class after the activity to hear some of students' reasons.

4 Read and complete the text message.

Students complete the past continuous sentences in the text message with the words provided.

Answers

1. listening, 2. talking, 3. eating, 4. watching,
5. having, 6. losing, 7. dancing, 8. playing

5 Read and circle the correct option.

Students review the usage of *while* and *when* with past continuous.

Answers

1. when, 2. while, 3. while, 4. when, 5. when

6 Complete the sentences using the correct forms of the verbs.

Students determine whether each sentence should be completed with the past continuous or past simple and write the correct form of the verbs provided.

Answers

1. raining, 2. saw, 3. started, 4. running, 5. trying

Extension

Students practice the past continuous by describing activities at home.

- Refer students to the text message description in Activity 4.

- Tell them to imagine a typical evening with their family and write about it as a past event. The information does not have to be true.

- When students finish, invite volunteers to read their descriptions to the class. Give anonymous feedback at the end.

Big Question

Students are given the opportunity to revisit the Big Question and reflect on it.

- Ask students to turn to the unit opener on page 69 and think about the question "How much do you remember?"

- Ask students to think about the discussions they've had on remembering, the readings they've read and the timeline they made.

- Students form small groups to discuss the following:
  - » *What's your earliest memory?*
  - » *Are there some things you will never forget?*
  - » *Do any of the elderly people in your life like to talk about their past? Why do you think this is?*

⭐ Scorecard

Hand out (and/or project) a *Scorecard*. Have students fill in their *Scorecards* for this unit.

▶ **Study for the unit test.**

83 ◀

6 What do you need to travel?

Grammar

Present Perfect: She <u>has had</u> a wonderful experience.
Present Perfect – *Ever*: <u>Have</u> you <u>ever been</u> to England?
Present Perfect – *Already, Yet*: He <u>has already made</u> some friends.
<u>Have</u> you <u>seen</u> anything interesting <u>yet</u>?

Vocabulary

Travel: book a flight, catch a train, exchange money, get a passport, hire a guide, pack a suitcase, stay in a hotel
Collocations: get hot, get hungry, get lost, get ready, get started, get there, get thirsty, get up

Reading

Reading images

Listening

Identifying images from descriptions

In the first lesson, read the unit title aloud and have students look carefully at the unit cover. Encourage them to think about the message in the picture. At the end of the unit, students will discuss the big question: *What do you need to travel?*

 Teaching Tip

Setting the Tone for the Lesson

Here are some tips to set the tone for a fun, but under-control learning environment:

- Don't allow food in the classroom unless it's a special occasion. Students finishing lunch or a snack will probably not be paying much attention to the lesson.
- Think of students as young adults. Adults can get bored or distracted, as well. Instead of getting frustrated with students, negotiate rewards for the class being focused, such as a timed break at the end of class or a favorite game.

 **Vocabulary**

Objective

Students will be able to use **personal experiences** and **keepsakes** vocabulary to talk about memories.

Lesson 1   Student's Book p. 84

Warm-up

Students look at photos of travel destinations to generate interest and activate prior knowledge.

- Bring post cards and/or photos of travel destinations to class, enough for each group to have four or five pictures.

- Students form groups. Distribute the travel photos and encourage students to guess the places. Monitor and give clues as needed.

- If time permits, tell students to exchange pictures with another group and continue the activity.

1 🎧²⁵ **Listen and mark (✓) the vacation destination.**
Students listen and mark the correct locations.

Answers

1. a busy restaurant, 2. a water park, 3. a beach

 86

Audio Script

1. [a busy foreign restaurant]
2. [a water park with kids splashing]
3. [a beach]

2 🎧²⁶ **Listen and number the activities.**
Students listen to the travel advice and number the activities in the order they are mentioned.

Answers

1. get a passport, 2. book a flight, 3. stay in a hotel, 4. hire a guide, 5. pack a suitcase, 6. exchange money, 7. catch a train

Audio Script

The world is full of amazing destinations where you can relax and explore at the same time! If you go abroad, first, you need to get a passport. It's a form of identification that says who you are and what country you're from. And you'll need to book a flight. Most people do it online. You can make a hotel reservation online, too. Choose carefully. You want to stay in a hotel that is safe and comfortable, but not too expensive. Hire a guide! The knowledge of a local guide is worth your money! On the day before the trip, pack a suitcase with the clothing you will need. Check the weather forecast and don't take too much stuff. When you arrive at your destination, exchange money. Make sure you do it in a formal exchange office and not in the street! Finally, if you can catch a train to get from one place to another—riding a train is one of greatest pleasures of traveling!

3 **Read the descriptions and write the travel activity.**
Students identify which travel activity from Activity 2 corresponds to each description.

- Draw students' attention to the *Guess What!* box. Read the information aloud. Ask students why they think those destinations are so popular and whether they would like to visit them.

Answers

1. get a passport, 2. book a flight, 3. pack a suitcase, 4. exchange money, 5. hire a guide, 6. stay in a hotel, 7. catch a train

Extension

Students do a role play activity related to travel activities vocabulary.

- Write a travel activity phrase in large letters on a sheet of paper. Do the same for the other travel activity phrases. Number the papers 1 through 7. Stick the papers in different areas of the classroom as activity stations.

- Have students count off by sevens and go to their corresponding station.

- Groups at the stations role-play their activity, for example, checking into a hotel or packing a suitcase. Each student should have a role in the role play, although they can be objects, too.

- After five minutes, have groups rotate to a different station and do a new role play. Repeat as time permits.

Wrap-up

Students review vocabulary with a matching activity.

- Write these locations on the board: *at home, at an airport, at a government office, at a station, at a travel destination.*

- Refer students to the vocabulary phrases in Activity 2. Ask *Where do you do each activity?*

- Students form groups and match the locations to the travel activities vocabulary phrases. Some activities have more than one answer.

- Elicit students' answers.

▐▐▶ **Workbook p. 146, Activity 1**

✔ **Homework Check!**

Workbook p. 146, Activity 1

Answers

1 Unscramble and match. Then look and number the photos.

1. hire a guide, 2. stay in a hotel, 3. book a flight, 4. catch a train, 5. get a passport, 6. pack a suitcase; *first column* 4, *second column* 6, 2, 1, *third column* 3, 5

Warm-up

Students review vocabulary with a game of *Bingo*.

- Elicit the travel activities phrases from the previous lesson and write the nouns from these phrases on the board, for example, *passport.*

- Draw a grid with nine squares on the board. In the center square, write *Free Space.*

- Have students copy the grid and write one noun in each space. They can use one word twice.

- Say the beginnings of the phrases for students to cross out the corresponding nouns. The first student with three in a row horizontally, vertically or diagonally should shout *Bingo!* Elicit the three phrases.

- Play several times.

4 Read and match.

Students read the text and then match the parts of the sentences.

Answers

1. a rock formation in Utah. 2. very early in the morning. 3. packed water and snacks. 4. because he got lost in the desert. 5. helped him find the destination.

5 Read again and underline the expressions with *get*. Then complete the dictionary entries.

Students underline expressions with *get* in the text in Activity 4 and complete the collocations.

Answers

1. hot out, 2. hungry, 3. lost, 4. ready, 5. started, 6. there, 7. thirsty, 8. up

6 Think Fast! Write five sentences using *get*.

Students do a three-minute timed challenge: they write sentences using the expressions with *get*.

Extension

Students brainstorm other collocations with *get*.

- Write the word *get* on the board.

- Elicit the collocations with *get* from the unit: *get hot out, get hungry, get lost, get ready, get started, get there, get thirsty, get up.*

- Students form teams of three or four.

- Set a stopwatch for one minute.

- Students race to see how many phrases they can think of that begin with *get*.

- After one minute, each team has one member write their phrases on the board. The team with the most correctly spelled phrases wins.

- Extend the activity by having students race against the clock to make sentences using collocations with *get*.

Wrap-up

Students play *Charades* to review collocations with *get*.

- Divide the class into three or four groups.

- One student in each group acts out a travel activity for the others to guess.

- Groups repeat with different volunteers acting out the vocabulary.

⟫ Workbook p. 146, Activity 2

87 ◀

Grammar

Objectives

Students will be able to use **present perfect** and *ever, already* and *yet* to talk about the present results of past actions.

Lesson 3   Student's Book p. 86

> ✔ **Homework Check!**
>
> Workbook p. 146, Activity 2
>
> **Answers**
>
> **2 Read and complete the sentences.**
>
> 1. thirsty, 2. up, 3. hungry, 4. ready, 5. there, 6. lost, 7. started

Warm-up

Students play *Two Truths and a Lie* to build interest in the topic.

- Write the following statements about Portugal on the board:

  » *The capital of Portugal is Lisbon.*

  » *Portugal has a population of 11 million people.*

  » *Portuguese is only spoken in two countries, Portugal and Brazil.* (LIE—*It's the official language in nine countries: Portugal, Brazil, Mozambique, Angola, Guinea-Bissau, East Timor, Equatorial Guinea, Cape Verde, and São Tomé and Príncipe.*)

- Tell students that two of the statements are true, but one is a lie.

- Students form pairs and guess which statement is the lie.

1 Read and number the photos.

Students read the brochure and match the points describing the program to the photos.

- Draw students' attention to the **Present Perfect** box and explain the use.

Answers

top to bottom 2, 5, 4

2 Complete the e-mail.

Students read the e-mail from a student interested in studying in Portugal and complete it.

- Draw students' attention to the **Guess What!** box. Read the information aloud. Ask students to choose someone in the class and ask about a life event.

Answers

(1) program at Jefferson, (2) I am studying, (3) to Portugal before, (4) heard a lot of, (5) My cousin did a, (6) send me

Extension

Students practice the present perfect with a game called *Find Someone Who.*

- Write *Have you ever...?* on the board. Elicit an example of the question from the brochure: *Have you ever studied or lived in another country?*

- Have students count off by sevens and go to their corresponding station.

- Elicit other ways to complete the question, for example, *eaten sushi, visited the US, played tennis, swum with dolphins*, etc.

- Tell students to write five questions with *Have you ever...?* Then have them ask other classmates the questions until they find at least one person who has done each activity.

Wrap-up

Students practice past participles with a ball toss game.

- Write two or three verbs on the board and elicit their past participles, for example, *see – seen.*

- Say another verb and toss the ball to a student. He or she should say the past participle. The rest of the class can help if needed.

- Then the student says another verb and tosses the ball to another student. Continue until all students have participated.

▶ **Workbook p. 147, Activity 1**

✔ **Homework Check!**

Workbook p. 147, Activity 1

Answers

1 Read and complete using *ever* and the present perfect.

1. Has he ever tried chai tea? 2. Has she ever gotten lost? 3? Have they ever taken a train? 4. Have you ever lived abroad?

Warm-up

Students practice the present perfect with *ever* with a game of *Ask, Don't Answer!*

• Ask *Have you ever…?* and encourage the class to complete the question.

• Divide students into large groups and have each group stand in a circle.

• Students should ask the person to their left a question with *Have you ever…?*

• Instead of answering, the student must immediately ask a new question. Questions cannot be repeated.

• If a student takes answers or repeats a question, he or she is "out." The last student in each group is the winner.

3 **Write the past participles of the verbs. Use the ad and the e-mail on page 86.**

Students identify the past participle of each verb. They can find the past participles in Activities 1 and 2.

Answers

1. studied, 2. lived, 3. made, 4. given, 5. been, 6. taken, 7. heard, 8. had

4 **Complete the sentences using the present perfect.**

Students form the present perfect of the verbs given as cues to complete the sentences.

• Draw students' attention to the ***Present Perfect: Already, Yet*** box and explain the difference between the use of both words.

Answers

1. have been, 2. has heard, 3. has lived, 4. has given

5 **Think Fast! In your notebook, write the past simple forms of the verbs in Activity 3.**

Students do a five-minute timed challenge: they recall and write the past simple forms of the verbs in Activity 3.

Answers

1. studied, 2. lived, 3. made, 4. gave, 5. was / were, 6. took, 7. heard, 8. had

6 🎧²⁷ **Listen and mark (✓) the correct option.**

Students listen to the conversation and mark the corresponding answers.

Answers

1. Jo's cousin, 2. 17, 3. Yes, he has. 4. No, he hasn't. 5. tried some unusual foods

---

Audio Script

JASON: Hello, Jo! It's Jason, your favorite cousin! Happy birthday!

JO: Thanks Jason. It's nice to hear from you.

JASON: I can't believe you're 17! Are you having a good birthday?

JO: Yes! My host family made me a cake and gave me a sweater!

JASON: How's it going in Portugal? Have you learned Portuguese yet?

JO: Yes, I have. I've already learned a few expressions!

JASON: How are things at school?

JO: Not bad. I study a lot, but I'm getting good grades.

JASON: And have you made any friends yet?

JO: A few. There's Fabio—he's Italian, and Sylvie, a French girl.

JASON: And what about Lisbon? Have you seen anything interesting yet?

JO: No, I haven't. But next week, we're going to St. George's Castle.

JASON: What's the most interesting thing you've done so far?

JO: I've already tried some unusual foods. I've had all kinds of traditional dishes.

JASON: It's sounds like you're having a great time, then.

JO: Yes! But I miss home. Say "hi" to everyone for me.

JASON: I will!

---

7 🎧²⁷ **Listen again and complete using *already* or *yet*.**

Students are exposed to the usage of *already* and *yet* with present perfect as they complete the sentences.

Answers

1. yet, 2. already, 3. yet, 4. yet, 5. already

Wrap-up

Students practice the present perfect and *already* and *yet* by completing sentences and questions.

• Write sentences or questions on the board, with a space replacing *already* and *yet*, for example, *Has Sara cleaned her room _____?*

• Have students complete them in their notebooks. Then elicit the answers.

➠ **Workbook pp. 147 and 148, Activities 2 and 3**

⏱ *Reading & Listening*

Objectives
Students will be able to read images and identify images from a text.

Lesson 5   Student's Book pp. 88 and 89

✔ *Homework Check!*

Workbook pp. 147 and 148, Activities 2 and 3

Answers

2 Look and write sentences using *already* and *yet*.

1. I have already taken pictures. 2. I have already watched a sunset. 3. I haven't eaten bobotie yet.
4. I haven't given a monkey bananas yet.
5. I haven't bought souvenirs yet. 6. I have already heard a lion roar.

3 Read and circle the correct option.

1. been, 2. gone, 3. gone, 4. been

Warm-up

Students have a competition to generate interest and activate prior knowledge.

- Write the words *TRAVEL DESTINATION* on the board.

- Students form groups of three.

- Set a stopwatch for three to five minutes.

- Students try to write as many words as they can with the letters in *travel destination*.

- The group with the most correctly spelled words when the stopwatch goes off wins.

1 **Look at the map and mark (✓) the correct option.**
Draw students' attention to the ***Be Strategic!*** box. Read the information aloud. Ask students to predict the content of the article base don the map.

Answers

1. destinations in a trip around the world.
2. in chronological order.

2 **Scan and complete the information on the map.**
Students scan the text looking for the information they need to complete the blanks on the map.

Answers

from left to right 64, New York, 79, Venice, 7, India

3 **Write 1, 2 or 3 to indicate the correct paragraph.**
Students identify the paragraph with the corresponding information.

Answers

1. 3, 2. 2, 3. 3, 4. 1

4 **Read and circle *T* (True) or *F* (False).**
Students determine whether statements about the text in Activity 2 are true or false.

Answers

1. F, 2. T, 3. T, 4. F (He used nineteenth-century forms of transportation.), 5. F (He traveled from Italy to Greece.), 6. F (It took 50 days to reach Japan.), 7. T

Wrap-up

Students discuss their opinions and thoughts on the reading.

- Write the following questions on the board:

  » *Have you, or do you know someone who has, ever visited the places Michael Palin went to?*

  » *What are some pros and cons of the way Michael Palin traveled?*

  » *Would you like to travel around the world? Why or why not?*

- Students form groups of three or four to discuss the questions.

- Come together as a class and have some students share their thoughts and ideas.

➠ **Workbook p. 149, Activity 1**

Teaching Tip
Managing Fast Finishers
Some students complete activities more quickly than others, so it's a good idea to have a few extra activities on hand, otherwise these students may become bored and disruptive. One set of activities designed for fast finishers are the *Just for Fun* pages. Students can work on these individually and then check their answers in the back of the Student's Book. The *Just for Fun* activities for this unit are on page 96.

✔ **Homework Check!**

Workbook p. 149, Activity 1

Answers

1 Look at the map and circle the correct option.

1. cities, 2. railway, 3. transportation

Warm-up

Students review the reading from the previous lesson.

- Write the names of the cities from the reading on the board in random order: *London, Venice, Athens, Alexandria, Mumbai, Madras, Singapore, Shanghai, Yokohama, Los Angeles, New York.*

- Invite volunteers to number the cities in the correct order.

- Ask students which city they would most like to visit.

5 🎧²⁸ **Listen and number the photos.**

Students listen to the interview and number the photos in the order they hear the topics mentioned.

Answers

1. [two men with headsets and headphones], 2. [the Eiffel Tower], 3. [skydiving], 4. [a sport event], 5. [a cardboard headset]

Audio Script

MALE PRESENTER (MAX): Today tech specialist Priya Advani of *Technology Today* is going to talk about virtual travel. Priya, welcome.
PRIYA: Thank you, Max.
MAX: What exactly is virtual travel?
PRIYA: Well, this is when you can experience a destination without physically being there.
MAX: Can you give us an example?
PRIYA: Sure. One way is with a special headset. You see an image through the headset, but if you turn your head, the image moves. It tricks your brain into believing you are at that place. And the headphones have a 360-degree sound profile of that location, too.
MAX: That sounds really interesting! What kind of places can you see?
Priya: Well, there are a lot of options. Some governments make virtual tours of famous landmarks in their country, to promote tourism. Imagine visiting Chichen Itza or the Eiffel Tower from your own living room! And people also create virtual simulations for training purposes—for example, you could practice skydiving without getting into an airplane! They are even making 360-degree recordings of sports events so that people can relive the action through virtual reality.
MAX: But can you buy one of these devices? They must be very expensive.

PRIYA: Yes… and no. You can turn your phone into a virtual reality device with a simple cardboard headset and regular headphones.
MAX: That is amazing! Do you recommend any websites where people can…?

6 🎧²⁸ **Listen again and circle the correct option.**

Students choose the words that correctly complete the sentences from the listening.

Answers

1. travel, 2. head, 3. virtual tours, 4. buy, 5. turn

Stop and Think! Criticak Thinking

What are the advantages and disadvantages of virtual travel?

- Draw students' attention to the photos in Activity 5.

- Ask *What is virtual travel?* Elicit or provide *when you experience a destination without physically being there.*

- Ask *Do you think you would like to travel virtually? Why or why not? What are the advantages and disadvantages of virtual travel?*

- Students form small groups to discuss.

- Invite a few students share their thoughts and opinions.

Wrap-up

Students play a timed geography game.

- Give students two minutes to write as many city names as they can. They get one point for each city in their own country, and an extra point if the city is in another country. The student with the most points is the winner.

- Have students write the city names on the board. Write the English versions of the names as needed.

▶ **Workbook p. 149, Activity 2**

Preparing for the Next Lesson

Ask students to watch an introduction to Sri Lanka: https://goo.gl/PPhje9 or invite them to look around on the web site: https://goo.gl/e2mH8q.

Culture

Objectives
Students will be able to talk about shipwreck diving and auto rickshaws in Sri Lanka.

Lesson 7   Student's Book pp. 90 and 91

> ✔ **Homework Check!**
>
> Workbook p. 149, Activity 2
>
> **Answers**
> **2 Read the article and match the numbers with their meaning.**
> *left column* 6, 1, 3
> *right column* 2, 5, 4

Warm-up
Students find Sri Lanka on a map.
- Have students keep their books closed. Display a world map.
- Tell students they can ask twenty *Yes-No* questions to identify the country you're thinking of, for example, *Is it in the Pacific Ocean?*

1 Read and match.

➤ 92

Students match the parts of the sentences to complete facts about Sri Lanka.

Answers
1. in the Indian Ocean. 2. flag in the world.
3. originated in Sri Lanka. 4. exporter of tea.
5. is volleyball. 6. rice and curry.

2 Read and mark (✓) the correct option.
Students read the article about shipwreck diving in Sri Lanka and answer comprehension questions.
- Draw students' attention to the **Guess What!** box. Ask students to read the information.

Answers
1. the island is near a major shipping route. 2. they are easy for divers to reach. 3. coral, fish and other marine life. 4. they are interested in history.
5. people salvage metal from the wrecks.

Extension
Students play a game called *Shipwrecked*.
- Draw a picture on the board of an island and a sinking ship or bring one in to show your students.
- Students form groups of four or five.
- Tell students that they have been shipwrecked on a deserted island. They must try to survive.
- Write the following questions on the board:
  - *What eight items (and only eight) will you bring?*
  - *What possible problems will you encounter?*
  - *How will you solve them?*
  - *What roles and responsibilities will each of you take on? How will you divide the work?*
  - *How will you make decisions?*
  - *What sort of laws will you have in place?*
- Groups discuss the questions.
- Have students share their answers with the class. Challenge students to share their rationale for their choices.

Wrap-up
Students quiz each other on a text.
- Draw students' attention to the reading in Activity 2 and the statements in Activity 3.
- Students form pairs and write ten quiz questions for other pairs to answer.
- Pairs swap quizzes and try to answer the questions. Challenge students to answer with their books closed.
- Sets of pairs meet and go over the answers.
- Come together as a class and have some students share their scores.

⇒ **(No homework today.)**

Warm-up

Students make a KWL Chart to review and preview the topic.

• Draw a KWL Chart on the board, similar to following:

What I Know	What I Want to Know	What I Have Learned

• Ask students to think about what they know about Sri Lanka and what they want to know. Elicit some ideas. Give students a few minutes to complete the chart. Have students set their charts aside to use at the end of the lesson.

3 🎧²⁹ **Listen and complete the notes.**

Students listen and complete the notes with information from the audio.

Answers

top to bottom three, two to three, cheaper, small, cities, very fast, pollution

Audio Script

In Sri Lanka, as in many countries in Asia, auto rickshaws are one of the most common forms of transportation. An auto rickshaw is a vehicle with three wheels, a metal body and a canvas roof. The driver sits at the front and there is a cargo or passenger space in the back. Many of them are taxis. They can carry two or three passengers. The auto rickshaw has many advantages. It's cheaper than a car. It's small enough to travel on narrow country roads, but works well in cities, as well. However, there are also a few disadvantages. They aren't very fast. The maximum speed is 50 kilometers per hour, but less when there are passengers. They also cause pollution and make a lot of noise. In Sri Lanka, people call auto rickshaws *tuk tuks*. Why? Because the motor makes a *tuk tuk* sound! *Tuk tuks* are the most popular form of transportation in the country!

4 🎧²⁴ **Read and answer. What do people in Sri Lanka call auto rickshaws?**

Students answer the question with specific information from the listening.

Answer

Tuk tuks

Stop and Think! Critical Thinking

What adventurous activities can world travelers do in your country?

• Students form groups of three or four.

• Say *Think of some adventurous activities travelers can do in your country.*

• Students brainstorm activities.

• Come together as a class and have students share their activities. Write them on the board.

• Have students vote on the top ten adventurous activities.

Wrap-up

Students update their KWL Charts.

• Students take out their KWL Charts from the *Warm-up* and update the information.

• Students form small groups of three or four and share what they have learned.

• Encourage students to discuss some of the following questions:

  » *What was the most interesting thing you learned?*

  » *What was the most surprising thing you learned?*

  » *Would you like to travel to Sri Lanka? Why or why not?*

• Come together as a class and have some students share their thoughts and ideas.

▐▐▐➡ **(No homework today.)**

💭 Teaching Tip

Eliciting Imagination in the Classroom
Students who are willing to use their imagination and think creatively are more willing to take risks, which is important for language acquisition. Here are some ways you can cultivate your students' imagination:

• Create an emotional connection to the topic. When the activity is meaningful to students, they will always be more engaged.

• Permit frequent discussion and interaction among students. Let students know that their opinions are valid and respected.

• Offer a safe, nonjudgmental environment and students will be more willing to try new ideas.

• Teach students to correct their mistakes without feeling embarrassed.

Project

Objectives
Students will be able to make a travel experience poster.

Lesson 9   Student's Book pp. 92 and 93

Warm-up
Students play a game of *Pictionary* to review travel activities vocabulary.
- Model the activity by drawing one of the vocabulary items on the board, for example, *catch a train.* You cannot speak or write any words; you can only draw pictures.
- The student who guesses comes to the board and draws another action.
- The student who guesses comes up to the board next.
- Continue until all actions have been reviewed or all students have had a chance to play.

1 Look and classify the activities for each destination.
Students write the activities under the corresponding destination.

 94

Answers

1. swim in the ocean, stay at a five star hotel
2. ride a horse, mine for gold
3. sail, find a treasure

2 🎧³⁰ Listen and mark (✓) the destination.
Students listen to the travel advertisement and identify the destination.

Answer

The Old West

Audio Script

Welcome to Colorado! When you arrive, you will get off the train. Our town is very small, but we have a hotel, a saloon and a general store. Farmers live outside the town. They have cattle and grow crops like corn and wheat. You'll see a lot of cowboys, too. And there are some miners who search for gold in the mountains. If you think you're lucky, you can mine for gold, too! You can ride horses here all day and explore the beautiful country. You will see hundreds of wild bison—the local people call them buffalo—and you can hear wolves howling at night.

3 Look at the Travel Experience poster on page 93. What is the destination?
Students identify the destination featured in the poster on page 93.

Answer

A jousting tournament in the Middle Ages

4 Read and circle the correct option.
Students read the travel poster and answer comprehension questions by choosing the correct options to complete the sentences.

Answers

1. historical, 2. jousting tournament, 3. one example, 4. mentions

Wrap-up
Students share their reactions to a text.
- Write the following questions on the board:
  - » *Would you enjoy the travel destination from the text?*
  - » *Have you ever visited a place with an important history? What was it? What did you do there?*
  - » *If you could visit a historical place, where would you go?*
- Students form small groups of three or four and discuss.
- Come together as a class and have some students share their thoughts and ideas.

Lesson 10 Student's Book pp. 92 and 93

Warm-up

Students analyze a travel poster to prepare for the project.

- Draw students' attention to the travel poster on page 93.
- Ask *What types of information does the poster give?* Elicit or provide one or two, for example, *places you can see, things you can do.*
- Students form pairs and analyze the content of the poster.
- Students should identify something similar to the following: *places you can see, things you can do, food you can eat, places you can stay, background of the place / activities.*

5 Design a Travel Experience poster.

Using the poster on page 93 as a model, students follow the steps to design and present their own posters advertising a travel experience.

The Digital Touch

To incorporate digital media in the project, suggest one or more of the following:

- Students can create a poster by dragging photos into a Microsoft Word document.
- Instead of a poster, students can promote their travel destination with a narrated slideshow with Smilebox, http://goo.gl/nBDzq.

Note that students should have the option to do a task on paper or digitally.

Extension

Students make a to-do list to plan a trip based on a travel poster or slideshow.

- Display students' posters in your classroom, or have students watch each other's slideshows.
- Have students imagine a trip to their destination or the destination in one of their classmates' posters.
- Have them make a "to do" list of preparations for the trip, for example: *get a passport, book a flight,* etc.
- Ask students if they have ever done any of these activities.
- If time permits, have students explore their travel destination online.

Wrap-up

Students present their travel posters and vote on the best.

- Students form groups of four or five. They present their posters to each other, showing their posters and talking about the trips.
- After all students in each group have presented their posters, each group votes on the best one. (Students cannot vote for their own poster.)
- The finalists from each group come up to the front of the class and present their posters.
- Students vote on the best poster.

Workbook p. 148, Activity 1 (Review)

Review

Objective
Students will be able to consolidate their understanding of the vocabulary and grammar learned in the unit.

Lesson 11   Student's Book pp. 94 and 95

> ✔ Homework Check!
>
> Workbook p. 148, Activity 1 (Review)
>
> **Answers**
>
> **1 Read and complete the e-mail.**
> up, ready, started, lost, hungry, hot, thirsty

Warm-up
Students brainstorm the language from the unit with a relay race.

- Students form three teams and line up in front of the board.
- Ask *How much can you remember from the unit?* Explain that they should write down as many vocabulary words, grammar examples, reading topics and listening topics as they can remember. Explain that each student can only write one item before passing the marker in relay fashion to the next student.
- Set a stopwatch for two or three minutes. Give the first student in each team a marker.
- Students race to write down the items from the unit.
- The team with the most correctly written items when the stopwatch goes off wins.

1 Look and complete the travel activities.
Students identify travel activities vocabulary presented in photographs.

Answers

1. book, 2. catch, 3. stay, 4. get, 5. hire, 6. exchange, 7. pack

2 Look and circle the correct option.
Students identify the expression with *get* represented in each photograph.

Answers

1. get hungry, 2. get there, 3. get thirsty, 4. get up

Extension
Students review travel activities vocabulary and collocations with *get*.

- Have students write each vocabulary item in a sentence.
- When they finish, have volunteers write their sentences on the board.
- Check students' sentences together with the class.

Wrap-up
Students review vocabulary with a game called *Categories*.

- Students form two teams, Team A and Team B.
- Assign each team a category, for example, for Team A, assign *travel destinations*; for Team B, assign *travel activities*. Students should not let the other team know their category.
- Teams meet for five minutes to make a list of ten items in their category.
- The teams write the first two items on the board. Then they try to guess the categories. If they guess right away, they win eight points, one for each unlisted item. If not, teams add another item to the board and guess again.
- The team with the most points wins.
- Play again, but this time, let teams choose their own categories.

➡ **(No homework today.)**

🗩 Teaching Tip
Encouraging Self-Correction

As students become more proficient in English, they may "catch" their mistakes as they make them. However, this is a difficult skill and students may need help to identify their mistakes. Here are some prompts you can use to quickly signal a mistake and foster self-correction:

- Agree with the class on an unobtrusive gesture, such as touching your nose or earlobe when there is a mistake.
- Gently repeat the error to elicit the correction.
- Prioritize the mistakes you plan to correct. For example, you can signal only errors related to the target language, or only errors that interfere with meaning.

You will probably need to be less strict with weaker students or students who are not confident, but more strict with students who are very fluent and frequently make the same mistakes.

Warm-up

Students review past participles.

- Invite several volunteers to write a verb on the board. When they finish, they should give their markers to other students for them to add new verbs to the board.

- Repeat the process, but have students write the corresponding past participles. They can use the *Verb List* on page 168 as a guide.

3 Look and write the past participle form of the verbs.

Students review the past participles of the verbs given.

Answers

1. eaten, 2. made, 3. taken, 4. given, 5. heard, 6. seen

4 Unscramble the sentences.

Students unscramble the words to form sentences in present perfect.

Answers

1. Bryan has been to Japan. 2. Karen hasn't studied for the test. 3. Have you ever written a letter? 4. Have you ever gone to a concert?

5 Look and write the sentences using the present perfect.

Students review forming sentences in present perfect using cues and *already* or *yet*.

Answers

1. We have already had lunch. 2. She has not been to the museum yet. 3. He has already taken the test. 4. They have not seen the movie yet. 5. Have you done your chores yet?

Extension

Students review with a game called *Shoot for Points*.

- Bring in balls or crumple up pieces of paper to make balls.

- Place the trash can in an area of the room where there is some space. Take some masking or colored tape and draw a line several feet away.

- Students form two or three teams. Give each team a ball.

- A member of Team 1 takes a shot, trying to get his or her team's ball into the basket. If the student does it, he or she gets a chance to answer a question or complete an item.

- If the student answers correctly, that team gets a point. If not, reuse the question later.

- Continue with different teams until all of the questions have been answered.

- The team with most points wins.

- Here are some questions and items you can ask:

1. *What's the past participle of…?*

2. *Name three things you need to do to travel to another country.*

3. *What's a collocation with get that means you can't find your way?*

4. *Complete the sentence: I need to ___ a guide for our trip.*

5. *Name two activities you can do on a tropical beach.*

6. *How many shipwrecks are there off the coast of Sri Lanka?*

7. *How many wheels does a tuk tuk have?*

8. *Explain what virtual travel is.*

9. *How long did it take Michael Palin to travel around the world?*

10. *What novel inspired Michael Palin to make his trip?*

Answers

2. get a passport, pack a suitcase, book a flight, exchange money, stay in a hotel, 3. get lost, 4. hire, 5. sail, swim in the ocean, 6. over 200, 7. 3, 8. experiencing a destination without actually being there, 9. 80 days, 10. *Around the World in 80 Days* by Jules Verne

? Big Question

Students are given the opportunity to revisit the Big Question and reflect on it.

- Ask students to turn to the unit opener on page 83 and think about the question "What do you need to travel?"

- Ask students to think about the discussions they've had on travel, the readings they've read and the poster they made.

- Students form small groups to discuss the following:

  » *How often do you travel? Where have you been?*

  » *What do you need to travel?*

  » *What has been your best trip? your worst trip?*

- Monitor, offering help as needed, particularly with vocabulary.

★ Scorecard

Hand out (and/or project) a *Scorecard*. Have students fill in their *Scorecards* for this unit.

▶ Study for the unit test.

Grammar

Might **and** ***Would***: I <u>might</u> take the Island Survivor course. I <u>might not</u> sign up this year. <u>Would</u> you eat a bug? Yes, I <u>would</u>. No, I <u>wouldn't</u>.

Present Perfect – *Never*: I'<u>ve never</u> been very adventurous. He'<u>s never gone</u> skydiving.

Vocabulary

Extreme Sports: kite surfing, mountain biking, rock climbing, skydiving, snowboarding, white water rafting

Adjectives: bored, boring, excited, exciting, interested, interesting, terrified, terrifying, thrilled, thrilling, tired, tiring

Reading

Understanding text organization

Writing

Classifying facts

How adventurous are you?

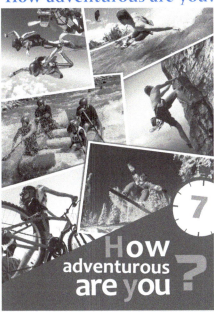

In the first lesson, read the unit title aloud and have students look carefully at the unit cover. Encourage them to think about the message in the picture. At the end of the unit, students will discuss the big question: *How adventurous are you?*

Teaching Tip

Dealing with Behavior Problems

All teachers must occasionally deal with behavior problems, such as class disruptions, unwillingness to participate in classroom activities and even bullying. Here are some things you can do:

• Be familiar with school policy, and refer students to specific rules as needed.

• Be consistent. Students are more likely to misbehave when they perceive that there are favorites, or when they know there won't be any consequences.

• Don't humiliate a misbehaving student. No one wants to be embarrassed in front of their peers. Talk with the student after class.

Vocabulary

Objectives

Students will be able to use **extreme sports** vocabulary and **adjectives** to talk about adventures.

Lesson 1   Student's Book pp. 98 and 99

Warm-up

Students make an acrostic to activate prior knowledge and generate interest.

- Write the word *ADVENTURE* vertically down the board. Model by writing a few words or phrases associated with adventure that begin with those letters, for example, *Awesome, Dangerous, Very interesting, Exciting…*

- Students form pairs and write acrostics.

- Monitor, offering help as needed.

- Come together as a class and have some pairs share their acrostics.

1 🎧³¹ Listen and number the extreme sports.

Students listen to people talk about their favorite extreme sports and number the photos in the order they are mentioned.

Answers

top row 6, 1, 3
bottom row 2, 4, 5

Audio Script

1. My name's Alexandra and my favorite sport is kite surfing. I live near the ocean, so I do it all the time. Basically, you have a surfboard and a special kite, and the wind pulls you over the waves. It's really thrilling—your heart beats fast and you forget about everything else.
2. I'm Kyle and I really like mountain biking! Most of the time I go on trails near my home, but sometimes I travel to the mountains. You see a lot of interesting places when you go mountain biking. I have a helmet camera, too, to make videos while I'm riding.
3. Hi. I'm Sarah and I'm into snowboarding. I travel to ski resorts all over the world. When I was younger, I was in a lot of competitions. Now I just do it for fun. It's never boring. Every mountain is different.
4. Hi. I'm Sam and I go skydiving. Actually, I've already jumped ten times and I want to become a skydiving instructor. My mom thinks skydiving is terrifying… She's extremely afraid of heights. But there's nothing like it in the world! For a few minutes, you feel like you're flying.
5. My name is Ron and I take people on white water rafting adventures. There are really difficult runs for experts, but there are also safer, calmer parts of the river for kids and families. It's exciting to be in the middle of a river navigating the currents.
6. I'm Emily and I'm into rock climbing. I started climbing in school, learning on a climbing wall. You have to train a lot, because climbing can be very tiring. If you run out of energy, you won't get to the top.

2 Look and write the name of the extreme sport.

Students look at the photos of sports equipment and identify the sports.

Answers

1. skydiving, 2. rock climbing, 3. white water rafting, 4. snowboarding, 5. mountain biking, 6. kite surfing

3 🎧³¹ Listen again and complete.

Students listen to the audio again and complete the sentences with adjectives from the box.

Answers

1. thrilling, 2. interesting, 3. boring, 4. terrifying, 5. exciting, 6. tiring

Wrap-up

Students practice the *-ing* participial adjectives from Activity 3 with a game of *Charades*.

- Model the game by acting out, without speaking, one of the participial adjectives, for example, *exciting*.

- Students form groups of four or five and take turns acting out the adjectives.

- Monitor, offering help as needed.

➡ **Workbook p. 150, Activities 1 and 2**

✔ **Homework Check!**

Workbook p. 150, Activities 1 and 2

Answers

1 Read and match to form extreme sports.
mountain biking, kite surfing, snowboarding,
white water rafting, rock climbing
**2 Read the descriptions and write the name
of the extreme sport.**
1. mountain biking, 2. snowboarding, 3. rock
climbing, 4. white water rafting, 5. kite surfing

Warm-up

Students review *-ing* participle adjectives.

• Ask volunteers to write the *-ing* participle adjectives
from Activity 3 on the board. Ask *What activities
are (boring)?*

• Students form pairs and give examples of activities
for each adjective. Invite volunteers to share their
ideas with the class.

**4 Think Fast! Describe the extreme sports using the
adjectives in Activity 3.**
Students do a three-minute timed challenge: they
write sentences combining the extreme sports with
the adjectives vocabulary.

Answers

Answers will vary.

5 Look and label.
Students identify the best adjective to describe
Stickman in each illustration. Point out the *-ed*
endings of the adjectives. Explain that these
adjectives describe feelings, not activities.

Answers

1. tired, 2. excited, 3. interested, 4. bored,
5. terrified, 6. thrilled

6 Read and match.
Students match the beginnings and endings of
sentences that explain how Jo is feeling in the
drawings in Activity 5.

Answers

1. he's waiting in a long line. 2. his favorite team is
winning. 3. a new book from the library. 4. a giant
spider. 5. winning a sports car! 6. he did a lot
of chores.

7 Think Fast! Complete the table.
Students do a three-minute timed challenge: they
complete the table to match the *-ing* participle
adjectives and the *-ed* participle adjectives.

Answers

left to right bored, exciting, interested, terrifying,
thrilled, tiring

Extension

Students practice participial adjectives with
a discussion.

• Write the following questions on the board:

1. *When was the last time you were terrified?*

2. *What is the most thrilling thing you've
ever done?*

3. *What do you do when you're bored?*

4. *What is something you find tiring?*

5. *What sport are you most interested in?*

• Students form small groups and discuss
the questions.

• Monitor, offering help as needed.

• Come together as a class and have a few
students share their thoughts and ideas.

Wrap-up

Students practice vocabulary with by playing
Criss-Cross.

• Write a vocabulary item on the board, for example,
white water rafting.

• Add another vocabulary item intersecting with the
first item like a crossword puzzle, for example,

> t
>
> i
>
> white water rafting
>
> i
>
> n
>
> g

• Invite volunteers to place additional vocabulary
until no more can be added.

➠ **Workbook p. 150, Activity 3**

Grammar

Objectives

Students will be able to use *might* **and** *would* **and present perfect with** *never* to talk about experiences.

Lesson 3 Student's Book p. 100

✔ **Homework Check!**

Workbook p. 150, Activity 3

Answers

3 Circle the correct option.
1. thrilling, 2. boring, 3. tired, 4. exciting,
5. interested

Warm-up

Students do a role play to demonstrate the meaning of a participle adjective.

- Students form small groups and choose a participle adjective. (Alternatively, assign each group an adjective.)

- Give them time to plan a role play. It should be a situation that can be described with the adjective.

- Invite groups to do their role play for the class. Then vote on the most entertaining role play.

1 🎧³² **Look at the Wild Adventures Survival Courses brochure. Then listen and circle *T* (True) or *F* (False).**
Students are exposed to *might* and *would* as they listen to two teens talking about the courses listed in the brochure. Then they answer comprehension questions.

102

Answers

1. T, 2. F (She might not sign up this year and she would take the Island Survivor course.), 3. T, 4. T, 5. T, 6. F (Megan will know next week if she can take a survival course.)

Audio Script

TYLER: Look, Megan! This is so cool. I did a survival course last summer in the desert. I loved it.
MEGAN: Oh, I saw that. I did the Junior Explorer course with my little brother last year. Which course are you going to do?
TYLER: Hmm. I haven't decided yet. I might take the Island Survivor course. Or I might take the Mountain Adventurer course.
MEGAN: I would do the Island Survivor course. It will be like being on vacation!
TYLER: Are you taking a survival course this summer?
MEGAN: I might not sign up this year. My aunt might take me on a trip to Spain.
TYLER: When will you know?
MEGAN: Next week.

Extension

Students make future predictions using *might*.

- Write different time references on the board: *tomorrow, next week, next year, in five years, in ten years.*

- Have students form small groups. Assign each group a time reference. Ask them to write three predictions about that time using *might*, for example, *It might rain tomorrow.*

- Come together as a class and have some students share their predictions.

Wrap-up

Students discuss the survival course from the brochure that they prefer.

➤ **Workbook p. 151, Activity 1**

🐝 Teaching Tip

Getting Results with Feedback

We know that providing students with meaningful feedback can greatly enhance learning and improve student achievement. It takes a lot of time and effort to provide students with good feedback. Here are some tips for getting results:

- Be as specific as possible. "Great job!" doesn't express what was correct, and likewise, "Keep trying!" doesn't indicate what to improve.

- Give feedback sooner than later. Feedback is most effective when it is given in the same activity or lesson, rather than a few days later.

- Involve students in the process. When students have access to their performance, they develop an awareness of their learning, and eventually, this can lead to self-correction.

✔ **Homework Check!**

Workbook p. 151, Activity 1

Answers

1 Look and write sentences using *might*.

1. I might take photos. 2. I might run 10 km. 3. I might visit the Butterfly Sanctuary. 4. I might get thirsty. 5. I might wear a life jacket.

Warm-up

Students review *might* for plans and predictions.

- Write six sentences with *might* scrambled on the board, for example, *might / pizza / tonight / some / have / I.*

- Give students two minutes to unscramble the sentences in their notebooks.

- Check by asking volunteers to write the unscrambled sentences on the board.

2 Read and mark (✓) about you. Then calculate your Survival IQ.

Students are exposed to the use of *would* as they read answer the quiz.

3 🎧³³ Listen and mark (✓ or ✗) the activities that each person has done.

Students listen to the conversation and mark the activities each person has and hasn't done.

Answers

Tara ✗, ✓
Mike ✓, ✗

Audio Script

MIKE: I brought that board game you like, *Have You Ever…?*
TARA: OK, Mike. What are the rules again?
MIKE: I ask you a question. You answer, but your answer might be a lie. I guess if you're telling a lie or not, and if I guess correctly, I win the card.
TARA: And if you guess incorrectly?
MIKE: You win the card.
TARA: OK. You go first.
MIKE: Have you ever… gone bungee jumping?
TARA: Yes! I went bungee jumping in February.
MIKE: Hmm. You're lying! You've never gone bungee jumping.
TARA: You're right. I've never gone bungee jumping. But it sounds like fun!
MIKE: OK. Your turn.
TARA: Have you ever… swum with sharks?
MIKE: No. I've never swum with sharks.
TARA: I believe you.
MIKE: You're… wrong! I swam with sharks on a trip last fall. They were really close to the beach and the lifeguard told everyone to get out of the water.
TARA: Wow! OK. So you *did* swim with sharks!
MIKE: Yep. OK. My turn. Have you ever… touched a spider?

TARA: No. No spiders. I've never touched a spider.
MIKE: Well, OK. I can believe that.
TARA: Hey! And you're wrong. My cousin has two pet tarantulas, and one time he let me carry it in my hand.
MIKE: Ew. So you have touched a spider, I guess, technically…
TARA: Yes. OK. Have you ever… seen a tornado?
MIKE: In real life?
TARA: Yes.
MIKE: No, I haven't.
TARA: You're… telling the truth.
MIKE: I am. I've never seen a tornado. But I'd like to someday. If I can see one from a safe place!

---

4 Write sentences about Tara and Mike using the present perfect.

Students write sentences about Tara and Mike's activities in Activity 3. They should use *never* in the negative sentences.

Answers

1. Tara has never gone bungee jumping. 2. Tara has touched a spider. 3. Mike has swum with sharks. 4. Mike has never seen a tornado.

5 Think Fast! In your notebook, write four sentences about things you have never done.

Students use present perfect to write about four things they have never done.

Wrap-up

Students ask each other about activities they have done.

- Form pairs and have them brainstorm and list ten adventurous activities. Each student should write the list.

- Form new pairs and ask each other questions using their lists of activities. Monitor, offering help as needed.

▮▮▮➡ **Workbook pp. 151 and 152, Activities 2 and 3**

Reading & Writing

Objectives

Students will be able to understand text organization and classify facts.

Lesson 5 Student's Book p. 102

> ✔ **Homework Check!**
>
> Workbook pp. 151 and 152, Activities 2 and 3
>
> **Answers**
>
> **2 Unscramble the sentences. Then look and number the situations.**
> 1. Would you travel in Europe by rail?
> 2. We would never live in Canada. 3. Would she ever go on a Jungle Adventure trip? 4. She would never go skydiving.
> *left to right* 3, 4, 1, 2
>
> **3 Look and complete using the present perfect and *never*.**
> 1. haven't, 've never gone diving, 2. haven't, 've never flown, 3. hasn't, 's never sung, 4. hasn't, 's never gone, 5. haven't, 've never been

Warm-up

Students preview photos to generate interest and activate prior knowledge.

- Write the following questions on the board:
  1. *What kinds of animals can you see?*
  2. *Where do you think they are?*
  3. *What do all the photos have in common?*

- Draw students' attention to the photos on pages 102 and 103.

- Students form pairs or groups of three to discuss.

- Monitor, offering help as needed.

- Come together as a class and have some students share their thoughts and ideas.

1 Look and classify the words.

Students read the ***Be Strategic!*** tip and practice classifying information by putting the words in categories.

Answers

Zoo Animals tiger, lion, elephant, zebra, *City Places* school, supermarket, museum, library, *Emotions* scared, sad, angry, happy, *Body Parts* face, hands, arms, feet

2 Read and number the headings.

Students identify the type of information in each paragraph and match each with the best heading.

Answers

2, 1, 3

3 Read again. Underline names of working animals and circle names of food animals.

Students classify pieces of information in the text, identifying the animals that are used for work and those used for food.

Answers

Working animals oxen, horses, mules, camels, elephants, dogs, reindeer, *Food animals* fish, buffalo, bison, mammoths, sheep, goats, cattle

Extension

Students do a classification task with real-world objects.

- Make a task kit for each group of students and place each in a large bag or shoe box: small plastic bags (for sorting), paper clips, note cards, rubber bands, brass fasteners, etc. There should be a few items for each possible "category." Mix everything together in each kit.

- Form groups and distribute the kits. One student will be blindfolded. He/She will take instructions from the rest of his/her group for sorting the objects into the small plastic bags.

- Display groups' organized kits. Elicit the categories they used. (Answers may vary.)

Wrap-up

Students do a classification task.

- Divide the class into small groups. Assign each group a category: *animals, occupations, countries, rooms in a house*, etc.

- Give groups two minutes to list as many words as they can in their category.

- Elicit one or two words from different groups and write them on the board in random positions. Then have several volunteers collect the word lists and copy them on the board in random positions. They should not group the words together.

- Give groups two minutes to read the words and identify the categories. When time is up, check answers with the class.

➠ **Workbook p. 153, Activity 1**

✔ Homework Check!

Workbook p. 153, Activity 1

Answers

1 Read the article and underline the adjectives that don't describe Bethany.

<u>unprofessional</u>, <u>terrifying</u>

Warm-up

Students are exposed to a topic with a game called *Two Truths and a Lie*.

- Write the following statements on the board:
  1. *The person who drives the dog sled is called the musher.*
  2. *Sled dogs usually weigh 30–40 pounds.*
     (LIE—They weight 50–60 pounds.)
  3. *Sled dogs love reindeer meat.*
- Students form pairs and decide which two are true and which one is a lie.
- Note how many pairs were right about the lie.

4 Imagine you need to add facts to the article. Circle the correct option.

Students identify which paragraph facts on each topic would fit in.

Answers

1. Paragraph 1, 2. Paragraph 2, 3. Paragraph 3, 4. Paragraph 1

5 Classify the facts for an article about sled dogs. Write B (Basic Facts) or H (History).

Students categorize facts for an article into basic facts and history about sled dogs.

Answers

1. B, 2. H, 3. H, 4. H, 5. B, 6. B

6 In your notebook, write two paragraphs about sled dogs using the facts in Activity 5.

Students use the facts they classified in Activity 5 to write two well-organized paragraphs about sled dogs.

Answers

Answers will vary.

Stop and Think! Critical Thinking

Is it OK to use animals for food and/or work? Why or why not?

- Remind students of the discussions they had in Unit 3 on vegetarianism and wearing fur. Ask them to share their opinions again.
- Then ask, *Is it OK to use animals for food and for work? Why or why not?* Ask students to say if there is a difference between eating and wearing animals and using them for work.
- Students form groups of three or four to discuss.
- Monitor, offering help as needed.
- Come together as a class and have some students share their thoughts and ideas.

Extension

Students research animals that humans use.

- Draw students' attention to the photos on pages 102 and 103.
- Elicit the types of animals that people are using in the photos: *camels, reindeer, horses, sled dogs.*
- Students choose one of the animals, either from the unit to research. You may also assign animals and have students work in groups.
- Here are some questions students can research:
  1. *How is the animal used?*
  2. *In which cultures or parts of the world is it used?*
  3. *How long has the animal been being used?*
  4. *Are there any ethical issues involved with the animal's use? Explain.*
- When students have completed their research, have them present what they learned to the class.

Wrap-up

Students share their sled dog paragraphs to consolidate the lesson.

- Have students take out the paragraphs they wrote in Activity 6.
- Students form small groups of three or four. They read each other's paragraphs, offering feedback.
- Students make edits to their paragraphs before forming new groups and taking turns reading them aloud to each other.
- Monitor, offering help as needed.

➠ **Workbook p. 153, Activity 2**

Preparing for the Next Lesson

Ask students to watch an introduction to Antarctica: http://goo.gl/aG1tkG.

Culture

Objectives

Students will be able to talk about Antarctica and the race to the South Pole.

Lesson 7   Student's Book p. 104

✔ **Homework Check!**

Workbook p. 153, Activity 2

Answers

2 Read again and underline the following information.

1. October 31, 2003, 2. Alana, 3. *Soul Surfer*, 4. World Surf League's Fiji Woman's Pro competition, 5. she wasn't considered a top surfer

Warm-up

Students play a game to activate prior knowledge and generate interest.

- Write *ANTARCTICA* on the board.
- Form small groups give them two minutes to make as many words as possible.
- Elicit students' answers.

1 🎧³⁴ **Read and guess. Then listen and circle the correct option.**

Students guess the correct option and listen to the audio to check their answers.

Answers

1. southern, 2. twice 3. ice, 4. desert 5. Summer 6. 4,000 7. dark

Audio Script

Antarctica is a pretty interesting place. It's a continent in the southern hemisphere. It's big—about twice the size of Australia. Ninety-nine percent of the continent is covered in ice, and that ice is 1.6 kilometers thick. But Antarctica doesn't get a lot of rain or snow. It's actually the world's largest desert. Since it's in the southern hemisphere, summer begins in December. No one lives in Antarctica permanently, but around 4,000 scientists live there in the summer months. Many of the scientists leave during the winter months when it is extremely cold and it is dark for 24 hours a day.

2 Look and label the map.

Students identify the continents and oceans on the map.

Answers

left side South America, Pacific Ocean
right side Africa, Atlantic Ocean, Indian Ocean, Australia

Extension

Students play a game similar to *Jeopardy*.

- Draw the following chart on the board:

Asia	Africa	Europe	North & South America
10	10	10	10
20	20	20	20
30	30	30	30
40	40	40	40

- Students form teams of four or five.
- They take turns choosing a category and a number. Ask the corresponding question. If they answer correctly, they win 10, 20, 30 or 40 points.
- Play until all items have been answered correctly. The team with the most points wins.
- Here are some items you can use:

Asia
100: This country has the largest population. (China)
200: It's the biggest country in Asia. (Russia)
300: The tallest mountain in the world is between Nepal and this country. (China)
400: This country used to be part of the British Empire. (Hong Kong)

Africa
100: The Great Pyramid is. (Egypt)
200: It's the longest river in the world. (the Nile)
300: This country is an island, and also the name of a children's movie. (Madagascar)
400: Nelson Mandela was from here. (South Africa)

Europe
100: You think of this country when you want to eat. (Hungary)
200: This country is the smallest one in the world. (Vatican City)
300: This country voted to leave the European Union in 2016. (the UK)
400: This country has part of its territory in Europe and part in Asia. (Turkey)

North & South America
100: This country covers about half of South America. (Brazil)
200: It's the second largest country in the world. (Canada)
300: This river carries more water than the world's other ten biggest rivers combined. (the Amazon River)
400: It's the world's largest island. (Greenland)

Wrap-up

Students make maps from the perspective of their country/countries.

▮▮▮➡ **(No homework today.)**

Lesson 8 Student's Book p. 105

Warm-up

Students guess the meaning of vocabulary with a game called Call My Bluff.

- Have students close their books.
- Write and number the vocabulary items from the listening on the board: *1. ultimate, 2. reach, 3. motorized, 4. supplies, 5. tragically*
- Students count off to form five groups.
- Assign one word for each group. Provide each group the definition for their vocabulary item; refer to the glossary on page 105.
- Tell students that they should think of another definition, one that might fool their classmates.
- Monitor, offering help as needed.
- Have groups read both definitions aloud. The other students try to call their bluff and say which definition is made up.
- You may also include other items from the text that you feel your students may have difficulty with, and add more groups.

3 Read the article and write A (Amundsen) or S (Scott).
Students read the article and identify which explorer each fact relates to.

Answers

1. S, 2. S, 3. A, 4. A, 5. A, 6. S, 7. A, 8. S

4 Underline the dates in the article. Then complete the timeline.
Students identify the dates in the text and use them to fill in the timeline.

Answers

left to right Oct 20, 1911, Nov 1, 1911, Dec 14, 1911, Jan 17, 1912, Jan 26, 1912

Stop and Think! Value

Is it OK for people to risk their lives in order to explore a place? Why or why not?

- Ask *Why do you think Scott and Amundsen risked their lives to get to the South Pole?*
- Elicit some answers.
- Then ask *Do you think it's OK for people to risk their lives in order to explore a place?*
- Students form small groups to discuss.
- Monitor, offering help as needed.
- Come together as a class and have a few students share their thoughts and ideas.

Wrap-up

Students retell a text using a timeline.

- Draw students' attention to the text in Activity 3. Ask them to tell you what they see in the photos.
- Draw students' attention to the timeline in Activity 4.
- Students form pairs and take turns retelling the text, using the timeline.
- Monitor, offering help as needed.
- Finish the activity with a round-robin. Write *In 1911, …* on the board.
- Have one student begin retelling the text, beginning with the phrase on the board.
- The next student continues to retell with another sentence. Then another student says a sentence and so on.

(No homework today.)

 Teaching Tip

Using a Cross-Curricular Approach in Your Classroom

Cross-curricular teaching involves a planned attempt to get students work with more than one academic subject simultaneously, for example, doing geography in an English lesson. There are many advantages to taking a cross-curricular approach. For one, it encourages students to think and reason, as well as transfer learning. Here are some tips for incorporating a cross-curricular approach:

- Find ways to integrate even minimal cross-curricular teaching into your lessons. For example, if a reading (as in the text in the *Project* page) talks about kilometers, consider integrating some math, covering measurements, into your lesson.
- Invite a guest to your classroom. In the case of this lesson, perhaps someone who has done something adventurous, like one of the extreme sports, or a geography teacher.
- Get artistic! Have students write a song, poem or short story with unit vocabulary.

Project

Objectives
Students will be able to make an Adventure Profile.

Lesson 9   Student's Book pp. 106 and 107

Warm-up
Students discuss their opinions to generate interest and personalize the lesson.
- Read the first sentence from the text aloud. Explain that this is sometimes called a *gap year*.
- Ask students if they know anyone who has taken a gap year, and if they think they would take one when they finish high school.
- Students form pairs and discuss the advantages and disadvantages of taking a gap year.

1 Look at the Adventure Profile on page 107. What was the adventure?
Students look quickly at the profile and identify the type of adventure the person featured went on.

Answer

cycling around the world

2 Read and underline the Adventure Profile facts in the article.
Students read the text and find the facts from the article that are given in the profile.

Answer

<u>Tom Davies</u>, <u>nineteen-year old</u>, <u>exercise in the gym</u>, <u>rode his bicycle on difficult terrains</u>, <u>France</u>, <u>Italy</u>, <u>Albania</u>, <u>Greece</u>, <u>India</u>, <u>Myanmar</u>, <u>Vietnam</u>, <u>Thailand</u>, <u>Singapore</u>, <u>Australia</u>, <u>New Zealand</u>, <u>United States</u>, <u>Canada</u>, <u>Spain</u>, <u>46,620 kilometers</u>, <u>food poisoning</u>, <u>bad weather</u>, <u>dogs</u>, <u>monkeys</u>, <u>youngest person to cycle around the world and he raised $80,000 for charity</u>

3 🎧³⁵ Listen and circle the correct option.
Students listen to the audio and circle the correct option to complete each fact in the profile.

Answers

Jessica, 38, million, Canada, Russian, astronaut, Mars

Audio Script
Did you ever want to be an astronaut and travel into space? Jessica Meir has wanted to be an astronaut since she was a small child. Now, she's 38 years old and she hopes to travel to Mars. If she is chosen for the mission, she will travel 54.6 million kilometers to the red planet. To prepare, Jessica studied in the US, France, Canada, Antarctica and Belize. In addition, she completed a difficult astronaut training program and learned Russian. Over the course of her career, she has become a marine biologist, a pilot and finally, an astronaut. She plans to accept any mission NASA gives her, and someday she might be one of the first humans on Mars!

Extension
Students discuss their dreams to personalize the lesson.
- Draw a bucket on the board and write *bucket list*.
- Explain to students that a bucket list is a list of things you haven't yet done but want to do in your life. (It comes from the expression *kick the bucket*, which is slang for *to die*.)
- Students form small groups to discuss what is on their bucket lists.
- Monitor, offering help as needed.
- Come together as a class and have some students share their thoughts and ideas.

Wrap-up
Students compare and contrast the adventure profiles to consolidate the lesson.
- Draw students' attention to the adventure profiles.
- Explain that when we compare two things, we find the similarities; when we contrast two things, we find the differences.
- Draw a Venn diagram on the board:

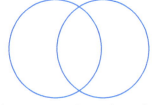

- Explain that in one circle, students should write facts about Jessica Meir; in the other, facts about Tom Davies. Where the two circles intersect, they should write what the two adventurers have in common.
- Students form pairs and compare and contrast the two profiles. Monitor, offering help as needed.
- Have pairs meet with another pair and share their findings.

⟫ **(No homework today.)**

Lesson 10 Student's Book pp. 106 and 107

Warm-up

Students brainstorm ideas about adventures to generate interest and activate prior knowledge.

• Draw students' attention to the icons in Activity 4.

• Students form pairs and say what adventure each icon represents.

• Draw students' attention to the headings in the profiles on pages 106 and 107.

• Students predict the information in the profiles, using the headings.

• Tell students that they will research one of the adventurers and learn the information.

◁ **Choose and research an adventurer. Make an Adventure Profile.**

Using the profiles on pages 106 and 107 as models, students choose one of the adventurers listed under Activity 4. They research the adventurer and use the facts they find to create an Adventure Profile.

The Digital Touch

To incorporate digital media in the project, suggest one or more of the following:

• Students can make their Adventure Profiles as PowerPoint presentations.

• They can also create a digital poster using Microsoft Word.

• More adventurous groups might make a podcast to accompany their Adventure Profile.

Note that students should have the option to do a task on paper or digitally.

Extension

Students watch videos on extreme sports to consolidate the lesson and initiate discussion.

• Show some videos on extreme sports: http://goo.gl/fnZKe5, http://goo.gl/b4rnyS and http://goo.gl/m2Ex88.

• Have students form groups and discuss the following after watching:

1. What is your opinion of each extreme sport?

2. Do you think you'd like to try one of the sports? Why or why not?

• Monitor, offering help as needed.

• Come together as a class, having a few students share their ideas and thoughts.

Wrap-up

Students get peer feedback on the content of their Adventure Profiles.

• Once students have gathered the information for their profiles, have them form small groups and explain their findings.

➤ **Workbook p. 152, Activity 1 (Review)**

🗨 Teaching Tip

Learning by Doing Tasks

When students do tasks, such as projects, they build their language skills in many ways.

• They use interactional language to plan and construct the project. This encourages students to think in English.

• They integrate target vocabulary and grammar with real-world information. Focusing on content helps students to internalize new language, rather than using it in a mechanical way.

• Students produce English based on ideas that are important to them. This gives students more motivation to use English clearly and correctly to express their ideas effectively.

• Tasks can help to make topics and new language more memorable, meaning they are more likely to remember and use the target language in the future.

 **Review**

Objective

Students will be able to consolidate their understanding of the vocabulary and grammar learned in the unit.

Lesson 11   Student's Book p. 108

✔ **Homework Check!**

Workbook p. 152, Activity 1 (Review)

Answers

1 Read and complete the sentences using participle adjectives.

1. interesting, 2. thrilled, 3. exciting, 4. tiring, 5. terrified

Warm-up

Students make a word scramble sheet for a classmate to complete.

- Write *skydiving* on the board with the letters scrambled, for example, *ydsnvkiig.*
- Elicit the vocabulary item and an example sentence.
- Have students scramble the remaining vocabulary items from page 98.
- Students form pairs and exchange lists. The first student in each pair to unscramble the words and write a correct sentence for each is the winner.

 110

1 Look and label the extreme sports.

Students review extreme sports vocabulary by identifying the sport in each photo.

Answers

1. white water rafting, 2. skydiving,
3. rock climbing, 4. kite surfing,
5. mountain biking, 6. snowboarding

2 Read and circle the correct option.

Students circle the correct participle adjective to complete each sentence.

Answers

1. terrifying, 2. tired, 3. thrilling, 4. excited
5. bored, 6. interesting

3 Complete the sentences using the unused words from Activity 2.

Students use the adjectives they did not choose in Activity 2 to complete the sentences.

Answers

1. exciting, 2. boring, 3. tiring, 4. thrilled,
5. interested, 6. terrified

Extension

Students imagine doing one of the extreme sports and make a word cloud with related words.

- Write the following words on the board in random positions, about mountain biking: *forest, trees, dirt, trail, morning, fresh, pines, bushes, sunshine, clouds, nature, fast, exciting, birds, wild,* etc. Some words can be written vertically.
- Give students time to read the words and ask about any unfamiliar terms. Elicit the sport.
- Form groups of three and have students choose a different extreme sport and create a word cloud. Encourage them to think about what they would feel, see, hear and even smell while doing the activity. Remind them to use different parts of speech such as nouns, verbs and adjectives.
- Have students display their word clouds around the classroom. Give them time to mingle and look at each other's work.

Wrap-up

Students practice participial adjectives with a competition.

- Write participle adjectives on notecards and stick them face-down to the board, so that students cannot see the words. They should be in random order. If possible, make more than one copy of each word.
- Divide the class into two or three large teams. Volunteers from each team take turns coming to the board and choosing two cards. If they match, they hold them up. Each team has one minute to discuss and write an example sentence. The sentence should be silly, for example, *Paul was very interested in butterfly recipes.*
- Give a point to each team with a correct sentence.
- Play several times, as time permits. The team with the most points at the end is the winner.

➠ **(No homework today.)**

Warm-up

Students practice the modals *might* and *would* with a game called *Flip and Roll*.

- Divide students into small groups and give each group a die and a coin.
- Write these options on the board:
  heads: *might*
  tails: *have never*

  1. fly in a plane
  2. go climbing
  3. eat a bug
  4. go skydiving
  5. swim with sharks
  6. see an alien

- Students take turns flipping the coin and rolling the die to determine what kind of sentence to make, for example, *heads* and *5* is *I might swim with sharks. Tails* and *1* would be *I have never flown in a plane.*
- Monitor and help as needed.

4 Read and correct the sentences.

Students practice usage of *might* by correcting the sentences.

Answers

1. ~~going~~ I might go to the gym this afternoon.
2. ~~to~~ We might not go to the party tomorrow.
3. ~~is~~ My family might travel to Spain this summer.
4. ~~has~~ She might have basketball practice after school.

5 Look and write the questions using *would*. Then answer about you.

Students form questions using *would* and the cues. Then they answer the questions with their own opinions.

Answers

1. Would you ride in an auto rickshaw?
2. Would you eat street food? 3. Would you go on a cruise? 4. Would you drink yak's milk?

6 Look and write about Gianna and Quinn using the present perfect and *never*.

Students write sentences in present perfect about the activities each person has never done using the information in the table.

Answers

1. Gianna has never failed a test. 2. Gianna has never gone sailing. 3. Quinn has never won a race.
4. Quinn has never taken a dance class.

? Big Question

Students are given the opportunity to revisit the Big Question and reflect on it.

- Ask students to turn to the unit opener on page 97 and think about the question, "How adventurous are you?"
- Ask students to think about the discussions they've had on travel, the readings they've read and the poster they made.
- Draw a scale on the board with the numbers 1 to 10, with a minus sign (-) under the 1 and a plus sign (+) under the 10.
- Ask, *How adventurous are you? Rate yourself on the scale.*
- Students form small groups to discuss the following:

  1. What was your rating on the scale? Did the result surprise you? Why or why not?

  2. Why do you think some people are more adventurous than others?

  3. Do you wish you were more adventurous? Why or why not?

- Monitor, offering help as needed, particularly with vocabulary.

★ Scorecard

Hand out (and/or project) a *Scorecard*. Have students fill in their *Scorecards* for this unit.

Study for the unit test.

8 What do we have in common?

Grammar
Too, Either: I like spicy food, <u>too</u>. / Me <u>too</u>. They don't like American food <u>either</u>.
So, Neither: I love horror movies. <u>So</u> do I.
I don't like sushi. <u>Neither</u> do I. / Me <u>neither</u>.

Vocabulary
Habits: go out to eat, hang out, keep a journal, order take-out, sleep in, stay up late, stream movies, work out

Listening
Identifying speakers

Reading
Reading a blog

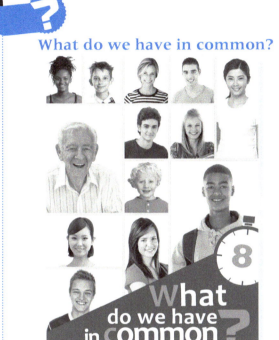

In the first lesson, read the unit title aloud and have students look carefully at the unit cover. Encourage them to think about the message in the picture. At the end of the unit, students will discuss the big question: *What do we have in common?*

🗨 Teaching Tip

Helping Students Consolidate Learning

Activities that consolidate learning help students reinforce what they have learned and also retain new material. Consolidation is an opportunity for you to clarify and address any doubts or trouble spots your students may have. It can also offer a chance for you to provide productive activities that personalize the lesson. Here are some activities for using consolidation to close a lesson effectively:

• Students list three things they learned in the lesson.

• Give students a 60-second challenge: Write down everything you can think of from the lesson.

• Brainstorm or mind map what was learned in the lesson, either in pairs, small groups or as a class.

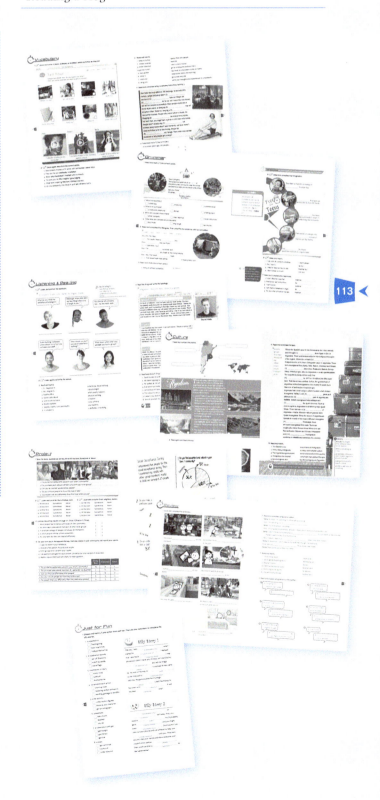

Vocabulary

Objectives
Students will be able to use **habits** vocabulary to talk about how they spend their time.

Lesson 1   Student's Book pp. 112 and 113

Warm-up
Display clocks and calendars (or photos of them) around the room. Write *How do you spend your time?* on the board.

- Students form pairs and answer the question, for example, I wake up at around six o'clock.
- Remind students to think about both school days and weekends.

1 🎧³⁶ Listen and write J (Jaya), B (Bryan) or M (Maia). Which activities do they do?
Students are exposed to daily routine vocabulary in a listening as they identify the speakers' habits.

Answers
first row J, M, J, B
second row M, B, M, M

Audio Script
JAYA: Hi! My name is Jaya and I live with my family in Washington, D.C. How do I spend my time? I'm in the drama club at school. At home, I stream TV series on my computer. My sister Adya and I stay up late—maybe until one or two in the morning—watching them. But only on the weekends. On school nights, we study and go to bed early.
BRYAN: Hi. I'm Bryan. I'm from Montana. My family has a cattle ranch, so I do chores in the morning before school—and even on the weekends. And I like to hang out with my friends after school. We play football or go horseback riding. I like to work out, too. Mostly I lift weights and ride an exercise bike.
MAIA: Hello. I'm Maia and I'm from Houston, Texas. My parents are both professors at the university so they're very busy, so we order take-out a lot. I love it when we order Chinese take-out. It's nice to be able to eat restaurant food at home. We go out to eat, too, but we usually only eat at restaurants on special occasions. Hmm. What else? I love sleeping in on the weekends, maybe until ten in the morning. I like listening to music. And I want to be a writer, so I keep a journal of my thoughts and experiences.

2 🎧³⁶ Listen again and circle the correct option.
Students identify the words that correctly complete the sentences about the listening.

Answers
1. sister, 2. weekends, 3. football, 4. lifts weights, 5. Chinese, 6. ten

3 Read and match.
Students match the vocabulary phrases with their definitions.

Answers
1. write your thoughts and experiences in a notebook, 2. watch online movies, 3. buy food at a restaurant to eat at home, 4. go to a restaurant and eat there, 5. go to bed very late, 6. sleep extra time in the morning, 7. exercise, 8. spend time with people

Wrap-up
Students review the target vocabulary by writing sentences about themselves.

- Tell students to write one example sentence for each vocabulary item. It should be a sentence that is true for them.
- When they finish, ask volunteers to share one of their sentences by writing it on the board.

▶ **Workbook p. 154, Activity 1**

🐝 Teaching Tip
Doing Listening Activities
Listening is often the most difficult skill for students learning English. Here are some tips to make listening activities easier for students:

- Remember to use prediction strategies when possible.
- Repeat the track or pause it at key points to give students time to process all of the information.
- Remind students that they do not need to understand every word.
- Keep the focus of the lesson in mind. In some cases, a listening activity is only meant to introduce new vocabulary or grammar, rather than to teach listening comprehension.

✔ **Homework Check!**

Workbook p. 154, Activity 1

Answers

1 Decode the names of habits. Then number the photos.

1. keep a journal, 2. go out to eat, 3. hang out,
4. order take-out, 5. sleep in, 6. stay up late,
7. stream movies
top to bottom 5, 7, 0, 2, 6, 4, 1, 3

Warm-up

Students review activities with a game of *Memory* to prepare for the lesson.

- Have students take out a piece of paper. Students cut or tear it into eight pieces.

- Have students count off by As and Bs.

- Draw students' attention to Activity 3. Student A should write the activities from the left column. Student B should write the definitions from the right column.

- Students form pairs, A and B, and shuffle their cards together. They place them facedown between them.

- Student A turns over two cards. If they match, that is, if the cards turned over are the activity and its corresponding definition, Student A keeps them. If not, Student A turns the cards over, keeping them in the same place, and Student B turns two cards over.

- Students play until all cards have been matched. The student with the most cards wins.

4 **Read and complete using vocabulary items from Activity 3.**

Students complete a text with the vocabulary words and phrases.

Answers

1. stream, 2. order, 3. go, 4. in, 5. journal, 6. out,
7. up, 8. work

5 **Read and circle *Y* (Yes) or *N* (No).**

Students answer comprehension questions about the text in Activity 4.

Answers

1. Y, 2. N, 3. N, 4. Y, 5. Y, 6. Y, 7. N, 8. N

6 **Think Fast!** Which activities do you usually do? Make a list in your notebook.

Students do a thirty-second timed activity: they list the activities they do.

Extension

Students create a *Find Someone Who* questionnaire to consolidate what they have learned and personalize the lesson.

- Draw students' attention to the activities in Activity 1.

- Write *Find someone who...* on the board.

- Tell students to list the activities and draw a line after each one, where they can write their classmates' names.

- Give students a few moments to look at the activities and think about or write the questions they will ask their classmates.

- Students stand up and ask each other questions using the activities.

- Monitor, offering help as needed.

- When students have finished mingling, have them get into groups to discuss what they found out.

- Come together as a class and have some students share what similarities and differences they have with their classmates.

Wrap-up

Students vote on their favorite *habits* activity.

➠ **(No homework today.)**

🐝 Teaching Tip

Teaching Verb Phrases

When teaching verb phrases, do everything possible to bring students' attention to the particles, or "little" words, that form the phrase. Students are likely to remember *sleep* or *stay*, but forget which word goes with it. Being exposed to verb phrases and repeating and producing them will help students to learn them. In addition, help students to associate the verb phrases with activities in their everyday lives by asking questions and talking about the target language in personalization activities.

Grammar

Objectives
Students will be able to use *too, either; so, neither* and *me too, me neither* to express similar opinions and circumstances.

Lesson 3   Student's Book p. 114

Warm-up
Students have a word race to generate interest.
- Write *Activities* on the board.
- Students form pairs.
- Set a stopwatch for two minutes.
- Students race to make as many words as they can using the letters of the word on the board.
- When the stopwatch goes off, students take turns reading out their words. As the words are read aloud, students cross them out.
- When all words have been read aloud, the student with the most correctly spelled words wins.

1 **Read and mark (✓) the correct option.**
Students read the welcome letter and answer comprehension questions about it.

Answers

1. summer camp, 2. a welcome ceremony,
3. other campers, 4. eat snacks

 116

2 **Read and complete the dialogues. Then underline the sentences with too and either.**
Students are exposed to usage of *too* and *either* as they complete the sentences with the words in the box.

Answers

meet, Where, from, Have, been, But; <u>I'm from Colorado too! I've never been here either.</u>

3 **Read and circle the correct option.**
Students identify whether *too* or *either* correctly completes each sentence.
- Students refer to the **Too, Either** box. Then, they read and circle the correct options to complete the dialogues.

Answers

1. too, 2. either, 3. either, 4. too

Extension
Students review *too* and *either* with drama.
- Invite students to suggest situations when people might use *too* or *either: arguing with a brother or sister, explaining achievements, having a friendly conversation,* etc.
- Students form small groups and plan a role-play to demonstrate three examples of *too* or *either.*
- Invite some groups to do their role-play in front of the class.

Wrap-up
Students practice *too* and *either* with a simple coin game.
- Form pairs and give each pair a coin.
- Students take turns making a general statement about themselves or their opinions, for example, *I have a lot of homework today.*
- The other student flips the coin. If it comes up heads, the student should agree by using *too* or *either.* If it comes up tails, they disagree: *I don't.*
- Monitor, offering help as needed.

⫸ Workbook p. 155, Activity 1

✔ Homework Check!

Workbook p. 155, Activity 1

Answers

Unscramble and write.

1. She often sleeps in. He does too. 2. I don't work out every day. She doesn't either. 3. She can't hang out with them today. I can't either. 4. Our English teacher is cool. Our math teacher is too. 5. They aren't happy with the football results. We aren't either.

Warm-up

Students review the rules for *too* and *either*.

- Write *too* and *either* on the board. Invite volunteers to explain when each is used.

- Form pairs and have them make a two-line dialogue for each.

- Come together as a class and have volunteers share their dialogues.

4 Think Fast! **In your notebook, write a dialogue using too and either.**

Students do a two-minute timed challenge: they write their own dialogues that include sentences with *too* and *either*.

5 🎧³⁷ Listen and complete the infographic.

Students complete the text about teens' habits with information from the listening.

Answers

2.5 or 2½, 72, 75, 4, 10

Audio Script

Did you know?

Teens listen to music for an average of two and a half hours per day.

Seventy-two percent of teens use social media to chat with friends.

Seventy-five percent of teens use social media or watch TV while doing their homework.

Teens spend, on average, only four minutes of free time per day reading.

Only ten percent of teens spend time outdoors on a regular basis.

6 🎧³⁸ Listen and match.

Students listen to a dialogue about the infographic and match the reply to each statement.

- Draw students' attention to the **So, Neither** box and read the information aloud.

Answers

1. So do I. 2. Neither do I. 3. I do too. 4. I don't either.

Audio Script

ELIZABETH: Wow, these statistics are really surprising. Only ten percent of teens spend time outdoors on a regular basis? I do a lot of outdoor activities.

JAYDEN: So do I: soccer, hiking, riding my bike… But I have friends who don't.

ELIZABETH: Do you use social media or watch TV while you're doing your homework?

JAYDEN: No, I don't.

ELIZABETH: Neither do I. What about reading? Do you read more than four minutes a day?

JAYDEN: Yes. I read at least an hour a day.

ELIZABETH: I do too. If you're a student, you read a lot.

JAYDEN: Ah! But it says "in your free time." Not school work.

ELIZABETH: Well… Uh… Do news articles count?

JAYDEN: Yes, I think so.

ELIZABETH: What about listening to music? We all do that, but I don't listen to music for two and a half hours a day!

JAYDEN: I don't either. I'm too busy. But I don't see a problem with it. It can be really relaxing.

7 Read and complete the responses.

Students determine which verbs to use to complete sentences with *so* and *neither*.

- Draw students' attention to the **Guess What!** box. Read the information aloud.

Answers

1. do I, 2. do we, 3. can I, 4. am I, 5. am I

Wrap-up

Students review *too, either, so* and *neither* with an opinions activity.

- Give students one minute to list five affirmative opinions, for example, *I think the school day should be shorter.*

- Give them another minute to write three negative opinions: *I don't think…*

- Form pairs and have them take turns reading and responding to the opinions using the target grammar.

➠ **Workbook pp. 155 and 156, Activities 2 and 3**

Listening & Reading

Objectives
Students will be able to **identify speakers** and **read a blog**.

Lesson 5 Student's Book p. 116

✔ Homework Check!

Workbook pp. 155 and 156, Activities 2 and 3

Answers
2 Read and number the lines of the dialogue.
2, 1, 7, 3, 0, 4, 5, 6
3 Write a dialogue for each photo.
Answers will vary.

Warm-up
Point out the **Be Strategic!** box for this unit and elicit the tips from previous units.

1 🎧³⁹ Listen and number the speakers.
Students listen and number the speech bubbles in the order they hear them.

Answers

first row 1, 2, 6
second row 3, 5, 4

Audio Script
DR. STEPHENS: Good afternoon. I'm Dr. Stephens, and today I'm here to talk about bullying. What do you think the definition of bullying is? Yes, you in the front. What's your name?
SOPHIE: Sophie Adams.
DR. STEPHENS: OK, Sophie. How would you define bullying?
SOPHIE: Bullying is when other kids say bad things about you or laugh at you.
DR. STEPHENS: Yes! Thank you, Sophie. There are many kinds of bullying, but one kind is when kids say bad things to you or about you, or when other kids laugh at you.
DUSTIN: Hi. I'm Dustin. I've read that some bullying is physical, when others try to hurt you or break your stuff.
DR. STEPHENS: Yes, you're right. It's very unfortunate, but bullying can be more than words.
MS. WAGNER: What about when other kids exclude you from a group? Ms. Wagner, by the way.
DR. STEPHENS: Yes, that's another aspect of bullying: excluding others, not letting them participate.
LYNN: Lynn Evans. I have a question. What should you do if you see or experience bullying?
DR. STEPHENS: Excellent question, Lynn. What should you do if you see or experience bullying?
MARTIN: Martin Skye. …Well, you should tell someone, but… no one really does.
DR. STEPHENS: Thank you, Martin. This is a very common problem. It can be embarrassing to talk to an adult about it. What if nothing changes? What if it makes things worse? But it does help. The best thing you can do is to stand up for others and include them. If you see bullying, be a friend. Now we're going to …

2 🎧³⁹ Listen again and write the names.
Students listen again and write the names of the speakers.

Answers

1. Dr. Stephens, 2. Sophie, 3. Martin, 4. Dustin, 5. Lynn, 6. Ms. Wagner

3 Read and match.
Students match to form statements about the speakers in the listening.

Answers

1. a psychologist. 2. a teacher. 3. a definition of bullying. 4. physical bullying. 5. what to do about bullying. 6. what usually happens. 7. are students. 8. to be a friend.

Wrap-up
Students discuss their reaction to the listening.
- Write the following questions on the board:
  » *What were the three definitions of bullying in the listening?*
  » *What is cyber-bullying?*
  » *What was the advice for what to do if you see bullying?*
  » *Was it good advice? Do you have any other advice?*
  » *Why do you think people bully other people?*
- Students form groups of three or four to discuss.
- Monitor, offering help as needed.
- Come together as a class and have some students share their thoughts and ideas.

➠ **Workbook p. 157, Activity 1**

Lesson 6   Student's Book p. 117

> ✔ **Homework Check!**
>
> Workbook p. 157, Activity 1
>
> **Answers**
>
> **1 Read and classify the adjectives.**
>
> *Jules* energetic, talented, stressed, casual
>
> *Ben* old, lonely, retired, hardworking, honest

Warm-up

Students test their knowledge about blogs to generate interest.

- Write the following questions and answer options on the board: (Answers are underlined here.)

  » Where was the first blogger from?
    a. *Germany*
    b. *China*
    c. *the US*

  » When was the first blog published?
    a. *1994*
    b. *2004*
    c. *2014*

  » How many blogs are there on the Internet?
    a. *1.5 million*
    b. *15 million*
    c. *1.5 billion*

  » How many bloggers blog full time?
    a. *2.7%*
    b. *27%*
    c. *72%*

  » What percentage of blogs are in English?
    a. *20%*
    b. *60%*
    c. *80%*

- Students form pairs and guess the answers. Then come together as a class and go over the answers.

4 Read the blog and write the headings.

Students read the text and identify the headings that best fit each blog entry.

Answers

I'm on the Team!, Whew! A Long Week,
A Big Move!

5 Read and circle *T* (True) or *F* (False).

Students answer comprehension questions about the blog.

Answers

1. F (He moved to a new city.), 2. F (His sister is going to the same school.), 3. T, 4. F (Some students made fun of his red hair.), 5. F (Jarred and his friends told other students to stop making fun of David.), 6. T, 7. T, 8. T

Stop and Think! Critical Thinking

How can friendship prevent bullying?

- Draw students' attention to Activity 1 on page 116. Remind them of the listening text.

- Ask students to think about the discussion questions in the Wrap-up in Lesson 5, especially the one on what to do if you see bullying.

- Students form small groups of three or four. Ask *Do you think that friendship can prevent bullying? How?*

- Monitor, offering help as needed.

- Come together as a class and have a few students share their thoughts and ideas.

Wrap-up

Students retell a text to consolidate their understanding of the content of the lesson.

- Draw students' attention to the statements in Activity 5.

- Elicit the correct information for the false statements. (See Answers for Activity 5.)

- Students form pairs and take turns retelling the text about David, using the statements in Activity 5.

- Monitor, offering help as needed.

 Workbook p. 157, Activity 2

Preparing for the Next Lesson

Ask students to watch a travel presentation about Argentina: http://goo.gl/qVHHY2 or invite them to look around the web site: http://goo.gl/I9yJp6.

 119

> 🐝 Teaching Tip
>
> **Setting up Respectful Group Discussions**
> Learning to communicate effectively is not easy, especially when it's on a difficult topic, such as bullying. Here are some tips for fostering effective communication, particularly when talking about sensitive issues:
>
> - Moderate conversations on sensitive topics. Establish rules for respect in group dialogue.
>
> - Promote active listening. Encourage students to take turns and make eye contact as they listen.

 **Culture**

Objectives
Students will be able to read and talk about Argentina.

Lesson 7   Student's Book p. 118

> ✔ **Homework Check!**
>
> Workbook p. 157, Activity 2
>
> **Answers**
> **2 Read, match and complete.**
> 1. a - e-commerce, 2. b - 70, 3. e - clothing,
> 4. c - common

Warm-up
Students discuss what they know about *Argentina*.
- Write *Argentina* on the board.
- Invite volunteers to say what they know about Argentina, for example, *It's in the Southern Hemisphere.*

1 Read and number the photos.
Students read the text about Argentina and number the photos to match them to the paragraphs.

Answers

left 4, 1
right 2, 3

2 Read again and label the map.
Students identify the places on the map.

Answers

left side Puna de Atacama, Patagonia
right side Iguazu Falls, Buenos Aires

3 🎧⁴⁰ Read and guess. Then listen and circle the correct option.
Students guess the words that complete facts about Argentina and then listen to check their guesses.

Answers

1. penguins, 2. Land, 3. cowboys, 4. drink,
5. The tango, 6. sugar

Audio Script
TEEN GIRL 1: OK. Are you ready? The topic is Argentina. Here's the first trivia question: Are there penguins in Argentina?
TEEN BOY: Penguins? Aren't they only in Antarctica?
TEEN GIRL 2: No, I read somewhere that there are penguins in South Africa, too.
TEEN BOY: OK, I'm going to say… Yes! There are penguins in Argentina.
TEEN GIRL 1: Let's see what the back of the card says… Argentina is home to Magellanic penguins. They are sensitive to pollution and climate change.
TEEN BOY: Woo hoo! I got one right!
TEEN GIRL 2: OK. My turn. What does Argentina mean?
TEEN GIRL 1: I don't know.
TEEN BOY: No idea.
TEEN GIRL 2: Argentina means "Land of Silver." Spanish conquistadors believed that the mountains of Argentina were full of silver.
TEEN BOY: Next. What are *gauchos*?
TEEN GIRL 1: I don't know. Boots?
TEEN GIRL 2: Uh, a type of food?
TEEN BOY: *Gauchos* are Argentinean cowboys.
TEEN GIRL 1: Oh! You learn something new every day, I guess. My turn. What is *yerba mate?*
TEEN BOY: Oh! I know this! We had some at school once. It's tea!
TEEN GIRL 1: *Yerba mate* is a traditional tea in Argentina.
TEEN BOY: Awesome!
TEEN GIRL 2: Name a dance from Argentina.
TEEN GIRL 1: Oh! Um… it's not salsa. What's the word…?!
TEEN BOY: Um, taco. No, tango!
TEEN GIRL 2: The tango is a famous dance from Argentina. Tango has European and African influences.
TEEN BOY: Yes! I think I'm winning! OK. Is the flavor *dulce de leche* popular in Argentina?
TEEN GIRL 2: I thought that was a Mexican thing.
TEEN GIRL 1: What's *dulce de leche?*
TEEN GIRL 1: It's made from milk and sugar and it's really sweet. You can put it on bread.
TEEN GIRL 2: OK, I'm going to say yes, then?
TEEN BOY: *Dulce de leche* is a popular treat in Argentina. It's also a popular flavor of ice cream!
TEEN GIRL 1: Pretty cool.

Wrap-up
Students quiz each other about Argentina to consolidate the lesson.
- Students form pairs and take turns asking and answering questions based on the text in Activity 1.

▐▐▐➡ **(No homework today.)**

Warm-up

Students make an acrostic to generate interest in the topic of the lesson.

- Write the word *ARGENTINA* vertically down the board.
- Elicit a few words that begin with the letters in ARGENTINA. There is no need to go in order.
- Students form pairs and use information from the Student's Book to make an acrostic.
- Monitor, offering help as needed.
- Come together as a class and have some students share their acrostics.

◁ **4 Read and complete the text.**

Students read the text about Argentinean history and culture and complete the sentences with words from the box.

Answers

1. people, 2. became, 3. Others, 4. million, 5. like, 6. important, 7. introduced, 8. President, 9. groups, 10. stores

5 Read and match.

Students match the beginnings and endings of sentences about the text.

Answers

1. the first immigrants to Argentina. 2. came from many parts of Europe. 3. was in favor of immigration. 4. a unique and complex culture. 5. enrich and transform the country.

Stop and Think! Value

What challenges do immigrants experience?

- Draw students' attention to the text in Activity 4.
- Have them locate the countries where Argentina's immigrants came from.
- Students form pairs.
- Ask, *What challenges did the immigrants to Argentina face?*
- Monitor, offering help as needed.
- Then ask, *Are they similar to challenges that all immigrants face? Explain.*
- Monitor, offering help as needed.
- Come together as a class and have some students share their thoughts and ideas.

Extension

Students prepare Argentinian food and drink.

- Draw students' attention to the statements in Activity 3 on page 118.
- Elicit some of the well-known food and drink mentioned in the listening.
- Students form small groups and choose one of the types of food or drink. They may also research other types of food and drink.
- Students either prepare the food or drink at home, or if possible, they prepare it in class.
- Have an Argentinian Food Fest day in class, where everyone shares their creations.

 121 ◀

Wrap-up

Students discuss which part of Argentina they would like to visit and why.

▐▐▐➡ **(No homework today.)**

Project

Objectives
Students will be able to conduct a *Social Acceptance* survey.

Lesson 9   Student's Book pp. 120 and 121

Warm-up
Students review the meaning of *all the time, sometimes* and *never.*
- Write the corresponding time expressions on the board. Invite volunteers to explain their meaning.
- Elicit example activities for each expression.

1 **Take the Social Acceptance Survey. Write *All the time, Sometimes* or *Never.***
Students answer the survey with their own information.

Answers

Answers will vary.

2 🎧⁴¹ **Listen and circle for Eva's brother, Josh.**
Students listen to a person answer the survey and record his responses.

Answers

1. All the time, 2. All the time, 3. Sometimes, 4. Sometimes, 5. Sometimes

 122

Audio Script

Eva: Will you take my survey, Josh?
Josh: I guess.
Eva: It won't take long. OK. You should answer *All the time, Sometimes* or *Never.*
Josh: OK.
Eva: Question 1. Do you feel accepted and valued in your town / community?
Josh: Uh, often?
Eva: Question 2. Do you make jokes about members of a particular social group?
Josh: You mean like making fun of people who are bad at sports? Yeah, all the time.
Eva: OK. Question 3. Can you be yourself around other people?
Josh: Oh, all the time.
Eva: Oh, your friends know that you sing in the shower? And have a huge playlist of love songs?
Josh: Uh, no. OK, OK. Sometimes I can be myself around other people.
Eva: Question 4. Do you criticize people for how they look or talk?
Josh: Well... I... I do. Sometimes. Like if they have cheap shoes or ... if they look overweight.
Eva: I see. OK. Question 5. Do people treat you differently than they treat other people?
Josh: I'd say... much better than they treat other people.
Eva: All the time, sometimes or never?
Josh: Sometimes. I mean, my teachers don't treat me better, but a lot of people at school do.

3 🎧⁴² **Listen and circle for Eva's neighbor, Amber.**
Students listen to a person answer the survey and record her responses.

Answers

1. Sometimes, 2. Sometimes, 3. Sometimes, 4. Never, 5. Sometimes

Audio Script

Eva: Thanks for helping me with my survey, Amber. It won't take long.
Amber: No problem. I'm glad to help.
Eva: Question 1. Do you feel accepted and valued in your town / community?
Amber: Hmm. Well, sometimes...
Eva: Only sometimes?
Amber: Yes.
Eva: Question 2. Do you make jokes about members of a particular social group?
Amber: Sometimes. But I try not to.
Eva: OK. Question 3. Can you be yourself around other people?
Amber: Sometimes.
Eva: Question 4. Do you criticize people for how they look or talk?
Amber: No. It's not right.
Eva: Question 5. Do people treat you differently than they treat other people?
Amber: Yes, sometimes.
Eva: I'm sorry to hear that.
Amber: What is this survey for again?
Eva: For school. Our unit is about how different people are... but the same, too.
Amber: That sounds nice. Good luck with it.
Eva: Thanks! And ... maybe we can talk again sometime.
Amber: I'd like that.

4 **Look at the survey results on page 121. Circle *T* (True) or *F* (False).**
Students answer comprehension questions about the survey results on page 121.

Answers

1. T, 2. F, 3. T, 4. T, 5. F

Wrap-up
In groups, students discuss their reactions to the example survey.

Warm-up

Students prepare to make a survey.

- Elicit question words and write them on the board: *How? Why? Who? When? What? Where?*

- Students form groups, the same groups they will be making their surveys with.

- Monitor as students discuss, offering help as necessary.

5 **Do your own Social Acceptance Survey. Interview people in your community and record your results.**

Students follow the steps to create and carry out their own survey about social acceptance. They use the model on page 121 to create a report of their results.

The Digital Touch

To incorporate digital media into the project, students can create their graphs with a word processing program such as Microsoft Word. Note that students should have the option to do the task on paper or digitally.

Extension

Students make a different graph for their survey.

- Draw students' attention to the graphs on page 121.

- Ask, *What kind of graph is shown?* Elicit *pie charts / graphs.*

- Brainstorm other types of graphs, for example, *bar graphs, line graphs, pictographs.*

- Have students get into the groups with which they made their surveys.

- Have students choose a different type of graph and create it based on the data they collected.

- Students present their graphs to the class.

Wrap-up

Students present their findings to the class to consolidate the lesson.

- Have one student from each group present his group's findings to the class.

- List the findings on the board, or assign a student to do so.

- When all groups have presented their findings, compare them.

- Encourage the class to draw conclusions based on the findings. Discuss, as a class or in groups, what they might say about social acceptance.

▮▮▶ **Workbook p. 156, Activity 1 (Review)**

Making Pie Charts by Hand

Technology can be very helpful for presenting information, but sometimes it is simpler or more appropriate for a group to do things "the old-fashioned way." Here are some low-tech tips for making pie charts:

- Have students use a compass to make the circle. Alternatively, they can trace a cup or some other circular object.

- Students can use an angle measure to divide the circle into 10 36 degree sections. They can also estimate this by dividing the circle in half and then estimating five equal sections in each half.

In addition, you may need to remind students how to calculate percentages for the survey: divide the number of people with a particular response by the total number of people surveyed.

123

 **Review**

Objective

Students will be able to consolidate their understanding of the vocabulary and grammar learned in the unit.

Lesson 11 Student's Book pp. 122 and 123

> ✔ **Homework Check!**
>
> Workbook p. 156, Activity 1
>
> **Answers**
>
> **1 Look and write a paragraph about their habits.**
> 1. Jo streams movies. Elsie hangs out with friends.
> 2. Jo sleeps in. Elsie stays up late. 3. Jo and Elsie keep journals. 4. Jo and Elsie work out.

Warm-up

Students review vocabulary with a game similar to *Pictionary*.

- Students form two or three teams.
- A student from each team sits with his / her back to
  the board.
- Write one of the activities from page 113 on
  the board.
- Students draw pictures to represent the actions. When a student with their back to the board guesses the activity, all teams stop drawing. The team that guessed correctly gets a point.
- A new student sits with his / her back to the board.
- Write another activity and students draw pictures to represent it.
- Continue until all activities have been reviewed.

1 Look and complete the sentences.

Students look at the illustrations and complete the corresponding sentences with vocabulary phrases.

Answers

1. go out to eat, 2. stream movies, 3. keeps a journal,
4. stay up late, 5. works out, 6. order take-out,
7. hang out, 8. sleeps in

2 Read and complete using *too* or *either*.

Students determine whether *too* or *either* correctly completes each sentence.

Answers

1. too, 2. either, 3. either, 4. too

Extension

Students practice vocabulary with a treasure hunt.

- Before class, write down the parts of each activity on two separate cards or sticky notes, for example, *stream / movies.*
- Stick them in different areas around the room.
- When students come in, set a stopwatch for one minute.
- Students hunt through the room, trying to match up the parts of the activities.
- The student with the most complete activities when the stopwatch goes off wins.
- Challenge students to make sentences with the activities they have.

Wrap-up

Students review *too, either, neither* by responding to statements.

- Have students take out a piece of paper and cut or tear it into four pieces.
- On each piece, students write a sentence. Here are some examples: *I'm studying Chinese.
  I'm going swimming this afternoon. I have two sisters.
  I love spicy food.*
- Students form groups of three.
- They put their cards together, shuffle them and place them in a pile in between them.
- The first student draws a card and reads the statement aloud. The other students respond, using *too, either, neither* or *so.* They take turns until all the cards have been used.
- Monitor, offering help as needed.

▶▶▶ **(No homework today.)**

Coping When Students Don't Understand

As teachers, we do our best for students to understand new grammar and vocabulary through careful presentation, a lot of practice and some opportunities to produce the new language. However, students sometimes need more time to grasp new language, especially with grammar concepts that are new or different from their first language. Try to be patient with students and offer additional explanations when needed.
Express confidence that students will understand it, even if they are having difficulty at the moment. Their continued interest and effort is more important than any one grammar point. Provide more practice, if possible, and if all else fails, focus on other areas of growth.

Warm-up

Students review *too, either, neither* and *so* with a mingle.

- Have students write 10 true statements about themselves. These can be about things they like and don't like to do, things they have or don't have, as well as things they're doing or would like to do.
- Monitor, offering help as needed.
- Write *Find someone who…* on the board.
- Tell students to draw a line after each sentence to write their classmates' names.
- Give students a few moments to look at their sentences and think about the questions they will ask their classmates.
- Students stand up and ask each other questions, using the statements on their papers.
- Monitor, offering help as needed.
- When students have finished mingling, have them get into groups to discuss what they found out.
- Encourage students to use *too, either, neither* and *so*, for example, *I don't like sushi and neither does David.*
- Come together as a class and have some students share what similarities and differences they have with their classmates.

3 Read and match.

Students review usage of *so* and *neither* by matching the appropriate response to each statement.

Answers

1. So do I. 2. So are we. 3. Neither can I.
4. Neither do I. 5. Neither am I. 6. Neither have I.

4 Read and answer using *Me too* or *Me neither*.

Students write responses to statements using *me too* or *me neither*.

Answers

1. Me too, 2. Me too, 3. Me neither, 4. Me too,
5. Me neither, 6. Me too

Extension

Students end the last lesson with a game called *Behind Your Back*.

- Write the expression *talk behind your back* on the board.
- Ask students if they know what it means. Elicit or provide *to talk about someone without that person being present*. Explain that the expression usually means negative talk, but today, we will talk positively behind each other's back.
- Tape a blank piece of paper on each student's back.
- Have them stand up, with only a pen, and mingle.
- Students mingle around the room, writing positive things about each other on the papers. You can join them.
- After several minutes, when students have had a chance to write their comments, they help each other get their papers from their backs and read the praise they received.

? Big Question

Students are given the opportunity to revisit the Big Question and reflect on it.

- Ask students to turn to the unit opener on page 111 and think about the question "What do we have in common?"
- Ask students to think about the discussions they've had, the readings they've read, listenings they've heard and the survey they made.
- Students form small groups to discuss the following:
  - » *What makes people different?*
  - » *Are there times when people's differences matter? Explain.*
  - » *There's an expression, "The world is getting smaller." What do you think that means? Do you think a "smaller world" makes people feel more or less different from each other? Explain.*
- Monitor, offering help as needed, particularly with vocabulary.

⭐ Scorecard

Hand out (and/or project) a *Scorecard*. Have students fill in their *Scorecards* for this unit.

➡ **Study for the unit test.**

125

Content Available on the Richmond Learning Platform

Worksheets

▼ Grammar Worksheets
- Stopwatch 4 Answer Key Grammar.pdf
- Stopwatch 4 Unit 0 Grammar 1 (4.0.G1).pdf
- Stopwatch 4 Unit 0 Grammar 2 (4.0.G2).pdf
- Stopwatch 4 Unit 1 Grammar 1 (4.1.G1).pdf
- Stopwatch 4 Unit 1 Grammar 2 (4.1.G2).pdf
- Stopwatch 4 Unit 2 Grammar 1 (4.2.G1).pdf
- Stopwatch 4 Unit 2 Grammar 2 (4.2.G2).pdf
- Stopwatch 4 Unit 3 Grammar 1 (4.3.G1).pdf
- Stopwatch 4 Unit 3 Grammar 2 (4.3.G2).pdf
- Stopwatch 4 Unit 4 Grammar 1 (4.4.G1).pdf
- Stopwatch 4 Unit 4 Grammar 2 (4.4.G2).pdf
- Stopwatch 4 Unit 5 Grammar 1 (4.5.G1).pdf
- Stopwatch 4 Unit 5 Grammar 2 (4.5.G2).pdf
- Stopwatch 4 Unit 6 Grammar 1 (4.6.G1).pdf
- Stopwatch 4 Unit 6 Grammar 2 (4.6.G2).pdf
- Stopwatch 4 Unit 7 Grammar 1 (4.7.G1).pdf
- Stopwatch 4 Unit 7 Grammar 2 (4.7.G2).pdf
- Stopwatch 4 Unit 8 Grammar 1 (4.8.G1).pdf
- Stopwatch 4 Unit 8 Grammar 2 (4.8.G2).pdf

▼ Reading Worksheets
- Stopwatch 4 Answer Key Reading.pdf
- Stopwatch 4 Unit 1 Reading 1 (4.1.R1).pdf
- Stopwatch 4 Unit 1 Reading 2 (4.1.R2).pdf
- Stopwatch 4 Unit 2 Reading 1 (4.2.R1).pdf
- Stopwatch 4 Unit 2 Reading 2 (4.2.R2).pdf
- Stopwatch 4 Unit 3 Reading 1 (4.3.R1).pdf
- Stopwatch 4 Unit 3 Reading 2 (4.3.R2).pdf
- Stopwatch 4 Unit 4 Reading 1 (4.4.R1).pdf
- Stopwatch 4 Unit 4 Reading 2 (4.4.R2).pdf
- Stopwatch 4 Unit 5 Reading 1 (4.5.R1).pdf
- Stopwatch 4 Unit 5 Reading 2 (4.5.R2).pdf
- Stopwatch 4 Unit 6 Reading 1 (4.6.R1).pdf
- Stopwatch 4 Unit 6 Reading 2 (4.6.R2).pdf
- Stopwatch 4 Unit 7 Reading 1 (4.7.R1).pdf
- Stopwatch 4 Unit 7 Reading 2 (4.7.R2).pdf
- Stopwatch 4 Unit 8 Reading 1 (4.8.R1).pdf
- Stopwatch 4 Unit 8 Reading 2 (4.8.R2).pdf
- Stopwatch Reading Worksheets Guidelines.pdf

▼ Vocabulary Worksheets
- Stopwatch 4 Answer Key Vocabulary.pdf
- Stopwatch 4 Unit 0 Vocabulary 1 (4.0.V1).pdf
- Stopwatch 4 Unit 0 Vocabulary 2 (4.0.V2).pdf
- Stopwatch 4 Unit 1 Vocabulary 1 (4.1.V1).pdf
- Stopwatch 4 Unit 1 Vocabulary 2 (4.1.V2).pdf
- Stopwatch 4 Unit 2 Vocabulary 1 (4.2.V1).pdf
- Stopwatch 4 Unit 2 Vocabulary 2 (4.2.V2).pdf
- Stopwatch 4 Unit 3 Vocabulary 1 (4.3.V1).pdf
- Stopwatch 4 Unit 3 Vocabulary 2 (4.3.V2).pdf
- Stopwatch 4 Unit 4 Vocabulary 1 (4.4.V1).pdf
- Stopwatch 4 Unit 4 Vocabulary 2 (4.4.V2).pdf
- Stopwatch 4 Unit 5 Vocabulary 1 (4.5.V1).pdf
- Stopwatch 4 Unit 5 Vocabulary 2 (4.5.V2).pdf
- Stopwatch 4 Unit 6 Vocabulary 1 (4.6.V1).pdf
- Stopwatch 4 Unit 6 Vocabulary 2 (4.6.V2).pdf
- Stopwatch 4 Unit 7 Vocabulary 1 (4.7.V1).pdf
- Stopwatch 4 Unit 7 Vocabulary 2 (4.7.V2).pdf
- Stopwatch 4 Unit 8 Vocabulary 1 (4.8.V1).pdf
- Stopwatch 4 Unit 8 Vocabulary 2 (4.8.V2).pdf

Class Audio
🎧 Track 1—Track 42

▼ Project Rubrics
- Stopwatch 4 Project Rubrics.pdf

▼ Scorecard ⭐
- Stopwatch 4 Scorecard.pdf

▼ Test

▼ Final Test
- Stopwatch 4 Answer Key Final Test.pdf
- Stopwatch 4 Final Test.pdf

▼ Mid-Term Test
- Stopwatch 4 Answer Key Mid-term Test.pdf
- Stopwatch 4 Mid-Term.pdf

▼ Placement Test
- Stopwatch Placement Test Answer Key.pdf
- Stopwatch Placement Test.pdf

▼ Standard Test
- Stopwatch 4 Answer Key Standard Test.pdf
- Stopwatch 4 Standard Test U1.pdf
- Stopwatch 4 Standard Test U2.pdf
- Stopwatch 4 Standard Test U3.pdf
- Stopwatch 4 Standard Test U4.pdf
- Stopwatch 4 Standard Test U5.pdf
- Stopwatch 4 Standard Test U6.pdf
- Stopwatch 4 Standard Test U7.pdf
- Stopwatch 4 Standard Test U8.pdf

▼ Test Plus
- Stopwatch 4 Answer Key Test Plus.pdf
- Stopwatch 4 Test Plus U1.pdf
- Stopwatch 4 Test Plus U2.pdf
- Stopwatch 4 Test Plus U3.pdf
- Stopwatch 4 Test Plus U4.pdf
- Stopwatch 4 Test Plus U5.pdf
- Stopwatch 4 Test Plus U6.pdf
- Stopwatch 4 Test Plus U7.pdf
- Stopwatch 4 Test Plus U8.pdf

Test Audio
🎧 Track 1—Track 8 Unit Tests
🎧 Track 9 Mid-Term
🎧 Track 10 Final Test

Verb List

Base Form	Past Simple	Past Participle	Base Form	Past Simple	Past Participle
become	became *	become	include	included	included
begin	began	begun	invent	invented	invented
believe	believed	believed	keep	kept	kept
blow out	blew out	blown out	laugh	laughed	laughed
book	booked	booked	learn	learned	learned
break	broke	broken	leave	left	left
build	built	built	make	made	made
burn	burned	burnt	open	opened	opened
buy	bought	bought	order	ordered	ordered
catch	caught	caught	pack	packed	packed
cause	caused	caused	paint	painted	painted
celebrate	celebrated	celebrated	plant	planted	planted
change	changed	changed	pollute	polluted	polluted
check	checked	checked	practice	practiced	practiced
collect	collected	collected	prevent	prevented	prevented
come	came	come	produce	produced	produced
complete	completed	completed	protect	protected	protected
conserve	conserved	conserved	provide	provided	provided
cry	cried	cried	put	put	put
dance	danced	danced	reach	reached	reached
decorate	decorated	decorated	receive	received	received
draw	drew	drawn	recycle	recycled	recycled
dress	dressed	dressed	reduce	reduced	reduced
drink	drank	drunk	relax	relaxed	relaxed
drop	dropped	dropped	remember	remembered	remembered
eat	ate	eaten	reuse	reused	reused
escape	escaped	escaped	save	saved	saved
exchange	exchanged	exchanged	say	said	said
exercise	exercised	exercised	see	saw	seen
explore	explored	explored	send	sent	sent
fall	fell	fallen	sleep in	slept in	slept in
feed	fed	fed	start	started	started
feel	felt	felt	stay up	stayed up	stayed up
find	found	found	stream	streamed	streamed
get	got	gotten	take	took	taken
give	gave	given	teach	taught	taught
go	went	gone	throw	threw	thrown
hang out	hung out	hung out	try	tried	tried
happen	happened	happened	turn	turned	turned
have	had	had	wave	waved	waved
hear	heard	heard	wear	wore	worn
hire	hired	hired	work out	worked out	worked out
improve	improved	improved	write	wrote	written

* Irregular verbs